SeminarBiz

How To Make Money in the Seminar Business

Dr. Bill Wittich

Knowledge Transfer Publishing

Knowledge Transfer Publishing
8650 Heritage Hill Drive
Elk Grove, CA 95624
www.volunteerpro.net
billwittich@comcast.net
916.601.2485

Ordering Information:
Quantity sales. Special discounts are available on quantity purchases by corporations, associations, and others. For details, contact the "Special Sales Department" at the address above.

How to Make Money in the Seminar Business / Dr. Bill Wittich. -- 1st ed.
ISBN 978-1-928794-04-2

This book is dedicated to the thousands of seminar attendees that have shared the seminar rooms with me and who continue to inspire me with their learning interest

CONTENTS

Introduction

Everyone is an expert on something and can teach what they know in a seminar

Everyone needs to learn something to improve their careers or even their everyday lives. They can visit a library or take a class at the local adult school. But for many people a short seminar that focuses on a very specific topic is the most cost and time efficient way to gain that new knowledge.

The focus of this book is to convince you that you are the best tool that this person has since you already have the information and people who are willing to pay for it. You can offer it in a clear and concise form without spending months sitting in a classroom. Taking a college or adult education class is not practical for many people since they do not need to spend 18 weeks to gain what they need to learn. Adult education and college classes are organized over a semester or quarter schedule because that is how it has always been done.

If you need to know how to build a website using WordPress, just how long would that take? Maybe a few hours to get you started? That is a perfect topic for a short seminar. As you gain knowledge you can sign up for a more advanced three-hour or a full-day hands-on seminar. The point is that a short seminar will give you the knowledge you need to start on that project.

Seminars come in many forms but the outcome is always the same, to help someone learn about a topic of interest to them in the shortest amount of time. The seminar might be held at a community college or in a hotel meeting room. This seminar might even be offered on a webinar that allows them to be in their office or even at home. It does not matter which format you use to conduct your seminar.

Your motivation might be to share your knowledge or that you are an entrepreneur wishing to start a new business. All seminars require strong organizational that is aimed at delivering knowledge in an efficient and cost-effective manner.

What is a Seminar?

Let's start by discussing just what the term seminar means. It does not matter if the seminar you develop is held in your own home or if you conduct a series of seminars across the globe. In all cases, planning is critical. Planning is required for the seminar to provide a meaningful learning experience. To your audience, your planning is invisible and truly all they care about is what they will learn. Time is a critical element in the adult learning arena. Your adult learner does not want to spend any more time than necessary to learn the solution to their issues.

Your seminar offered in the public arena will give you instant credibility. During a live seminar you have a captive audience who are attending to gain knowledge. This is knowledge that you will be delivering face-to-face to them. While all social media, from Facebook to Twitter can share knowledge, there is something special about spending time one-on-one with an instructor. During your seminar you are the rock star with all the information that people need to learn. It is a win-win environment for both your attendees and you. It allows you to offer them information during the seminar that will allow them to take you home. It may sound funny to say "take you home," but many of your attendees want to have additional tools from your tool kit. It allows you to offer a variety of other learning venues for them. These venues might include seminars, books, videos, podcasts, blogs, and webinars. These tools will give them more information and give you additional income.

Most people have attended college or adult education classes where the instructor presented material for eighteen weeks. Maybe after eight weeks you had all the information you came to gather, but the class still met for another ten weeks. The class went on for the full eighteen weeks because that was the schedule. You also realized that the instructor started covering material that was not critical but you realized that the class was required to go on for the full eighteen weeks. You could stop showing up for the class, but you felt that as a good student, you should finish the entire class. If you did not finish the class you would not receive the certificate.

This book will give you the keys to producing a seminar that provides information, excites your audience and makes you income for your efforts. It will take time and dollars to do it right, but it will be a fun and meaningful experience. This seminar could be an in-person event, an online teleseminar or a virtual webinar. All three forms are effective and require a similar planning process. It is important to discuss all the steps to planning a seminar. These steps will cover everything rom discovering the right topic to filling all the seats in your seminar room. Discovering the right topic depends on what you know and are willing to learn and what information your audience requires meeting their learning goals.

The key is to produce a quality seminar while spending the least amount of money.

A seminar, if it is to be a quality learning experience, must present critical information in the shortest amount of time.

This is why seminars are called short courses. The key is to offer your participants exactly what they need and no more. They are willing to give you their time and money to gain the desired information that they require.

Producing a seminar is both a business and a performance. Which of these two is most important, the business or the performance? The answer is that both are equally important because you must have a competent business plan and a meaningful event before you will attract a number of attendees.

Let's examine your experiences at the last seminar you attended. It was probably held in a hotel meeting room. You showed up fifteen minutes before the scheduled start time and someone checked you in. Thank goodness there was coffee, both regular and decaf. You didn't have time to stop at your local Starbucks because the traffic was unreal. You found a seat in a cold room, probably too cold and you wished you had brought a sweater. There were already a number of people sitting there and they were fairly friendly. You started a conversation with the person next to you and discussed what you knew about the presenter.

The presenter then started, a few minutes late with her welcome, and she gave an overview of the seminar. For the next three hours, you heard about a topic that was of interest to you or your boss. The presenter offered to meet with everyone following the seminar. She handed out a page with helpful references to resources on the topic of the seminar. She mentioned a follow-up seminar being held next month and offered a discount if you signed up today.

There was a large selection of books and videotapes available to purchase. These were on a table in the back-of-the room, and they were very visible as you exited the seminar room. One book written by the presenter covered today's topic in detail and you used your credit card to purchase it. The presenter was willing to sign the book and you took advantage of that offer. Sound familiar? Everyday there are thousands of seminars like this held all over the world on a wide variety of topics. Our task is to assist you in designing a seminar that you will present.

Every day, every evening, and all weekend long thousands of people attend either personal interest or business seminars. They attend because the topic is of personal interest to them or their boss suggested that it might be helpful with their position at work. The seminar might be called a short course, a seminar or even a workshop. It could be an on-line event that they can view at home, in the office or even at the local coffee shop.

How Do People Select a Seminar?

Generally speaking, people search for a seminar to attend based on their personal or companies' interest. They might hear about a seminar or find it on-line and they start planning to gather more information on it. They are concerned about where it is offered, how much time it requires and what it costs. The location is critical as that is both a time factor and a cost factor. If the seminar is located a distance from them it might require time off of work and transportation. If it is more than a few hours, it will require approval from their boss to miss time from work. The price of the seminar will require approval from someone since we all have limited funds for an educational experience. The higher the seminar fee, the longer it takes people to decide to attend. It may depend on who is paying for the seminar. If the participant is paying for the seminar, it will require them to decide if it is worth their attending. If their employer is paying, it might depend if the employer has a training budget for this purpose. If the attendance depends on the boss's approval, then the person will need to sell their boss on the value of the seminar.

While people purchase books or audiotapes on the spur of the moment, seminars usually require a longer time for the approval to attend. This might be because it will require the attendee to miss work or family time, or it may be simply a budget item. In ether case, it may require talking it over with the office or their significant other to insure that the funding and/or time is going to be available.

Is it a Seminar or a Workshop?

Are we talking about a seminar or a workshop? There is no universal definition for these two terms, but let's start by defining the seminar. Paul Karasik in his book *How to Make it Big in the Seminar Business* tells us "a seminar is an exchange of information that is confined to a specific topic." Howard Shenson in his book *How to Develop & Promote Successful Seminars & Workshops* says "seminars are particularly attractive because they communicate knowledge quickly and in an organized and strategically capsulated form." Herman Holtz in his book *Expanding Your Consulting Practice With Seminars* tells us "the distinguishing features of a seminar are a specialized subject and a relatively short duration."

It appears then that a seminar is a short event where people sit and listen to a presenter or a series of presenters discuss a topic of interest to the audience. The audience might take notes or even record the seminar. This seminar format is effective for those learners who learn by listening and watching someone do a task or explain a process.

A workshop is more interactive with the audience having a hands-on experience where they get to practice what the presenter illustrates. It is this hands-on aspect that is the difference between a seminar and a workshop. But to be honest, many people label their event as a workshop even though it does not involve the audience producing anything during the event.

A seminar and a workshop are live events where the attendees travel to a site and sit with others to watch a presenter. In today's digital world we need to add a third version, the virtual seminar. In the virtual event you learn without physically being there. You might be sitting at your desk or in your home while attending a virtual seminar. The virtual seminar might be presented globally and have an unlimited number of attendees. Unlike face-to-face seminars, virtual seminars do not require people to travel to a local site.

A critical difference in selecting between a seminar, a workshop or even a virtual event is the learning style of the individual. Some people learn faster by doing something rather than just hearing about it. You might enjoy taking cooking classes and the classes may vary between watching the chef demonstrate the preparation of a dish or where you are a participant in a hands-on class. You might love either, because in one session, you capture the passion of the chef telling stories while they cook and in the workshop you get to actually prepare the dish. A virtual cooking class might resemble your watching a Food Network show, but with the advantage of being able to question the chef.

The term short course could apply to either a seminar or a workshop. But to attract the right audience, you need to put a clear description into your marketing materials. You would need to be clear whether you are offering a seminar or workshop. It is wrong to have your prospective attendee think it is a hands-on workshop when it is really a seminar. That would frustrate them and your reputation would suffer. It is equally important to inform your attendees if you are offering a virtual seminar, rather than an in-person seminar. There is nothing wrong with a virtual on-line seminar, but you must be clear that is a virtual seminar and not an in-person one.

Why Do People Attend Seminars?

It is important to discuss why people attend seminars. We know that some people take the less expensive way of learning about a topic by buying a book. But with the cost of technical books these days the actual cost to attend a seminar and the cost to purchase a book might be fairly close. In fact, you might find many seminars are less expensive than a book. For many people the real value of attending a seminar is the opportunity to hear from the expert and to be able to ask questions of that person.

Equal to having the expert handy is the fact that you get to network with a large variety of other participants in the seminar room. These people might be much more knowledgeable on this topic than you are and they might serve as an additional resource. With these new friends you have an opportunity to brainstorm about your ideas and share your experiences. You will likely get a differing viewpoint from the presenter. For many attendees the seminar might be a tax write-off if it is in their business field. For others it might meet a continuing education requirement and qualify them for required CEU units.

Seminars allow you to be introduced to one or more industry leaders in a short amount of time. They also allow you to network with people who share a similar interest. A seminar allows you to get answers to your pressing concerns and to share your thoughts with others in the room. You will also gather current materials from the presenter as well as have the opportunity to purchase materials on the seminar topic.

Don't be surprised if many of your attendees are attending to meet friends or just to have an enjoyable evening out. I have attended a few of the *Meet-Up* or *Learning Annex* seminars and found that many people are there to have a fun experience by sharing a social time with friends. Nothing wrong with people having a social agenda and learning something at the same time.

Seminars are for Adult Learners

In this book the term seminar applies to both seminars and workshops, live and virtual. These events are different but in many ways they are similar. Both are intended for adult learners, rather than for students working on earning a degree. Adult learners are typically defined as learners over the age of 24 and are often referred to as nontraditional students. Adult learning is generally thought of as lifelong learning. Most lifelong learning occurs outside the formal classroom.

Adult learners are self-directed which means they have taken the responsibility to have control over their learning. They are practical and want content that can be immediately put to use in their lives. They do not want theory unless it relates directly to something they can apply. Their maturity as adults might indicate that they are less open-minded and more resistant to accepting new viewpoints. Therefore as the presenter you will need to stress the "why" behind all new concepts and techniques you plan to introduce.

It is important to realize that adult learners have high expectations. They want to be taught things that they can apply as soon as the seminar is complete. Adult learners have no patience for a seminar presenter that speaks down to them. Time is a major concern to adults and they do not want anything in a seminar that resembles busy work. One critical point with adult learners is that they will not stand to have their time wasted.

Many seminars are held after work hours and it is important to realize that your attendees have worked all day and are feeling tired. You need to exhibit your excitement and motivation to keep your audience with you. They are also juggling seminar attendance with work, family, and the cost of your seminar.

To adults a college class might appear to be covering unnecessary material. But remember that the average college class is required to meet for three hours a day for eighteen weeks. The professor may have completed all the required material in 15 weeks but still has to cover something for those remaining three weeks. They may consider telling the students that everything was completed for the course and they could leave and go enjoy themselves for the next three weeks. Their dean would not have had a good feeling about that. A seminar only needs to be as long as the subject matter requires.

Adult learning theory states that everything you are teaching must be distilled down to the essentials and that your participants must be able to apply your information upon leaving the seminar room. It tells us that adults are internally motivated and self-directed in their learning. Being self-directed, they bring life experiences into the seminar room. Adults want to be given an opportunity to use their existing knowledge and experience that they have gained from their life experience.

Adults are ready to learn when they experience a need to learn and generally not before that. They want to know the relevance of what they are learning to what they want to achieve. In other words, do not waste their time on meaningless exercises. Your participants need to feel that they gained information in the shortest amount of time.

It is critical for you to realize that a three-hour or even a six-hour seminar goes fast.

Many beginning presenters plan way too much material for the seminar and they find themselves with an hour or more of material left at the end of the session. You may find that your attendees ask so many questions that there is not enough time to cover the seminar content. You need to plan your seminar time to cover both seminar content and the question and answer session. You need to be aware that students want to ask questions, and this requires time. But you must prevent people from taking up too much time and throwing the entire seminar off schedule. You might tell your people that you will cover that topic later or that you are willing to meet them during break time or after the seminar to give detailed answers.

What is the Seminar Business All About?

Thinking business is an attitude that all seminar promoters need to develop. Too many people feel that a seminar is a quick road to wealth. Yes, you can earn a fair amount of income from the seminar business, but it is not instant money. The keys to success in the seminar business are to design a meaningful topic and to think marketing. The topic must be one that people are willing to give both the time and money to attend. The marketing is finding ways of attracting people into your seminar. Regardless of whether you are using other people's money (OPM) or investing your own capital, it is important to insure that a large number of people are interested in attending your event.

The Key to Your Business Plan

The key to your business plan must include a successful seminar that you can repeat in multiple locations on multiple dates. In the seminar business we call that rolling out your seminar. A single seminar offered once will give you enough income for you and your significant other to enjoy a weekend away, but your goal is to produce a continuing income source. The primary work will be in marketing your seminar, whether it is offered live or online. Conducting the seminar might be fun, but only if somebody signs up for it.

Developing your topic is another way of asking the question, what are you going to talk about? This is the biggest fear of those who are thinking about developing a successful seminar. It is not the fear of speaking in public. It is the fear of finding a topic that that people are willing to pay to attend. It must also be the topic that you know enough about to offer a three-hour seminar about.

Everyone has a topic that interests them. It might be learning more about wine. It might be how to survive teen-agers. It could be how to buy a car without being taken for a ride.

The key to the best topic is one that you have narrowed down to the bare essentials.

Your audience wants the key steps or the secrets to that topic. They do not need a college course on the topic. If they do, then they should sign up for an eighteen-week college semester on that topic. They are looking to know just the essentials. They hope that it can be done in three hours, or maybe in a full-day seminar. They want to walk away from your seminar feeling that they have the learned the essentials of that topic.

The topic you select must be one that either you are an expert on or that you are willing to burn the mid-night oil learning about. It must be a topic that has a large enough group of people interested in and willing to pay to learn more about. It has to be a general topic to attract a wide enough audience in a number of locations. This is because you plan to roll it out to multiple locations.

Your topic must be one that you are excited about because

you will spend months developing a seminar on this topic. Unless you feel motivated about it, nobody else will. Remember it is your attendees who will ultimately decide if you have a good topic. If no one signs up to attend your seminar, it is a good sight that you have not selected the right topic. Of course, it might be that you are charging too much to attend the seminar, or even that you are charging too little.

People expect to attend a seminar and go home with all the knowledge, skills and answers they need. They expect you to be the expert who can answer any and all the questions they have. They could simply go on line and find many of the answers to their issues, but they feel it is faster and easier to come to you. After all, you must be the person with all the answers, since you are teaching the seminar. That certainly scares some potential presenters and might even be giving you a headache or two. The answer to this concern is simply, do you have the time and the interest to do all that research on your topic? Is your material up to date? Nothing is more embarrassing than have an audience know more up-to-date information than you do.

The Content is Critical

Is your topic one that can be broken down in multiple sub-areas? It might be that your topic is too broad in nature. You might be a financial planner and you are planning to produce a seminar on financial planning. But your audience is looking for retirement planning or how to make money in the stock market, or they want tax planning advice. Any of these topics would be a killer topic for difference audiences. You need to focus your topic down to what your audience wants. Maybe you need to be more specific, not more general. You might focus on the needs of recently retired women who want to find a home-based business. You might aim your seminar at recently divorced stay-at-home moms who want a business aimed at other stay-at-home moms.

Find a topic that has direct benefits to the people signing up for your seminar. Remember that people do not buy seminars; they buy the benefits that the seminar offers. Take a look at the number of seminars being offered in relationship building. These seminars might be a way for people to spend a fun evening out meeting people. It might be an opportunity to meet other moms with young children or for those seeking to share an evening over a glass of wine with new friends. The theme might be hearing about the latest books or movies. Your challenge is to determine just what benefits your audience is looking for.

Your first task is to find a topic that people need and want.

The topic might be finding a new tool for their career or maybe a passion that they want to explore in more depth. The topic is the key to why people sign up to attend a seminar. You need to find a topic that people are willing to pay to obtain. This is the tricky part of the seminar business; since that topic might change year to year and it will often vary by location. You need to go inside your own head and see what topics you have a strong interest in producing a seminar about. If you don't have a strong interest in a topic, you will not be effective with it, or at the very least you will not enjoy spending time planning and researching it.

If you are a member of a service club like Rotary or Lions and you serve in membership recruiting, you probably have a strong interest in recruiting members. You know there are thousands of service clubs and that all these clubs have a need to find new members. You wonder if this might be a strong enough topic to fill a seminar room. So you go online and check out service club membership on Google and search for similar seminars. Then you search Amazon.com to see how many books are in print and how recent they are. Are the books all ten years old? What if you find only a few books on the subject or that the ones on the list are all outdated? It might indicate that you have found a strong need or it might indicate that there is not a lot of interest in this subject.

Let's talk about that for a minute. If you see a limited number of seminars on a subject, what does that tell you? Does it say that nobody has a need for that topic or does it say you have found a gold mine? Hard to tell, but either way it will require additional research. Then you could start by networking with a few membership organizations to see if they show interest.

Maybe you could offer your seminar on-site for a membership association. They could be willing to pay you a fee to present the seminar. This would mean they would do the marketing to attract attendees. The organization would supply the attendees and also pay your expenses for travel and lodging. If the membership associations you contact show an interest in a seminar, you might consider producing a seminar that a variety of association members would be interested in attending.

What if you have a topic that you feel is strong, but you are not up to date on this subject? If you have excitement about this topic, you may have found a fun way to spend a few months developing it into a seminar. If you live with a topic for a few months and search the Internet you will literally become an expert on it. Most seminar topics by nature are specific, but can only go into limited depth. Any seminar can cover only so much material in 3 to 6 hours. If your attendees desire additional knowledge on this topic, they will search out another seminar and/or purchase your back-of-the-room learning materials.

I recently produced a seminar titled *How to Deal with Difficult People.* You will probably agree that this is a topic that has universal appeal. All of us know about this topic having experienced a few difficult people in our lives. My research on this topic started with reading books, spending time on the Internet, and conducting numerous interviews with human resource experts. This research gave me a fairly complete list of the difficult people found in most organizations. This list helped me to outline the characteristics of each group of difficult people. Next was developing various techniques of handling each group. This hopefully led to successful methods of handling each group. It turned out that a large number of people desired this information. A seminar was produced both as an on-site offering for corporate clients and also as a public seminar. Since we can find difficult people everywhere, this topic had a wide audience appeal.

Research is Critical

Just don't assume that you have all the information and that no additional research is required. There is always more information to be found for any seminar. This was certainly true with my seminar on *Risk Management for Non-Profits*. I considered offering this seminar since I had authored a popular book titled *A Model Volunteer Handbook. This book* was published and for a number of years was considered useful to various non-profit groups. But when I started to design this seminar, I was amazed to find how the topics of youth protection, volunteer background screening and electronic liability had changed. In other words, the book was out-of-date. The good news is that my current research allowed me to offer a seminar and to rewrite the book as well.

Your audience will assume you are the expert on the seminar topic.

Your attendees will consider you to be the expert. They will think of you as an expert on this subject just because you are teaching the seminar. Experts all have opinions on their subjects and your audience wants to hear what your opinions are. Your audience could simply purchase a book on that topic, but they enjoy being able to gain your opinion.

Your opinions are a major reason they are attending your seminar. Don't feel that you should not give them that added feature. Remember that a book or even the Internet will not give them your opinion about the subject. Even though the seminar presents unbiased information, your audience wants to know what your opinion is. They want to know what works and what don't work. Many presenters' are hesitant to express their opinions in a seminar. I think that is a mistake. Your attendees are curious about your opinion.

Just because you are interested in a topic does not mean it is a lucrative subject for a seminar. People attend seminars because they have a strong interest in or a need for that topic. The topic must be of interest and be needed by enough people or you will be presenting to a very small audience and earning very little income. The size of the potential audience might determine just how much you charge for the seminar. If you have a topic required by a small number of people for their business you will have to charge a higher fee. If you are offering a subject that they are required to attend and you are one of the few people offering it, you have a strong topic.

Continuing Education Units

A continuing education unit is a measure used in continuing education programs, particularly those required in a licensed profession, for the professional to maintain the license. Examples of people who need CEUs include teachers, interior designers, architects, engineers, emergency management professionals, school administrators, educators, nurses, mental health professionals, and social workers. Generally, a CEU is defined as ten hours of participation in a recognized continuing education program, with qualified instruction and sponsorship. CEU records are widely used to provide evidence of completion of continuing education requirements mandated by certification bodies, professional societies, or governmental licensing boards. The records also provide employers with information on training pertinent to particular occupations.

The term CEU is in the public domain. You may award a CEU without requiring any accreditation. With a CEU an employer or other organization must decide on an individual basis whether to honor the CEU from training providers. The International Association for Continuing Education and Training (IACET) developed the continuing education unit (CEU) in 1970 and is the caretaker of the CEU. IACET assumes responsibility for refining and disseminating information about the CEU through its programs, publications and research. The CEU created by IACET is used by thousands of organizations. Only providers that go through the **Authorized Provider accreditation process** and get approved are allowed to issue IACET CEUs.

Every topic must be targeted to a very specific audience.

A few topics will fit a large group of potential attendees. Seminars on health and wellness might fit a wider audience because people are interested in being healthier and fit. Topics might be gender specific as well. Many seminars are aimed at women only while others will focus on a male audience. *SkillPath* offers a *Conference for Women*, which covers communication and conflict management skills for women. They advertise this conference as a conference designed to help women develop themselves professionally and to find fulfillment in everything they do! The attendees will spend the day with inspiring professional women trainers and network with women who are facing the same life situations.

CarrerTrack Seminars is offering a *Communication Skills for Women* seminar in a wide variety of locations. They state that this seminar is developed specifically to meet the needs of today's workingwoman and it offers valuable insights the audience can use to enhance their communication style while earning the respect and cooperation of others.

It is a good idea to begin collecting seminar brochures and reviewing seminar Internet sites. You will learn from companies who are successful in this business. You will be viewing seminar topics that run season after season. You will see which cities and hotels are being used by the seminar pros. Request to be added to the mailing list for Fred Pryor, Career Track, American Management Association, and your local community colleges. Scan these brochures and Internet sites on a regular basis to see what other seminar firms are offering. This will give you many ideas for topics and locations. They have put many dollars and hours into that research and you might as well take advantage of that. Believe me, these companies search each of their competitor's materials on a regular basis and you should do it as well.

A key requirement is to select a topic that contains hard to find information. If your seminar topic is in-demand and contains information that is hard to find, you might have a winner. We know that most adults are looking for instant solutions to their problems. Everything tends to be instant these days, from fast food to movies out of a Redbox. If your seminar is a no-pain, easy to use solution to their problem, you will find people standing in line to attend it.

What are a few questions for you to ask about your proposed seminar topic?

1. Is there a large enough audience that cares about or needs your topic?

    This is your potential audience that you are asking about. Without people who need your topic, you are not going to have a successful seminar. Just how big is this group of people who care about this topic? Just how big does it need to be? If you are offering your seminar through a community college, they will have a minimum number of attendees before they will agree to offer the seminar. They will also have a maximum number based of the size of the rooms available. If you are offering it yourself, you hopefully can find a larger facility if the attendance grows. Since with your own event your income is based on attendance you will want to have a minimum number of registrants before you offer the seminar.

If you experience a small number of attendees you might still want to offer the seminar if you have non-refundable airline tickets and hotel meeting room space that can not be cancelled at the last minute. The audience certainly gets value since they had to share the presenter with so few other people. It also allows you to promote the fact that you do not cancel your seminar because of low enrollment. That tends to be an incentive to help people enroll since they don't have to worry about the seminar cancelling. You might only cancel a seminar if no one showed up.

2. Will the potential audience retain their interest for a minimum of three years?

   The seminar business requires that you produce one seminar and be able to repeat it a number of times. It is not a one-shot dream. If you cannot repeat it regularly, then the cost is too high. You spend months getting the seminar ready to take on the road. You see professional seminar companies offering the same seminars all over the globe because they have a winner. It is the repeat seminar with limited revision costs that produces a winning seminar.

Many seminar topics have a limited time span. If you look at professional seminar catalogs for the past few years they will feature very difference topics. But a few topics would still be there. Customer service, communication skills, and team leadership would still be there in today's brochure. But even a few years ago most social media topics would be missing. Back then nothing on Facebook marketing, LinkedIn, or Twitter would be found.

Your research involves finding what topics have been around for the past few years. Then you will need to decide if they are going to remain viable for the next few years. This is difficult, but even if many of these topics are attracting less people, many of them can be revised with new sub-topics to make them work.

3. Is your audience fairly easy to find?

    Where are your prospects and how will you find
    them? This is your hidden gold mine. It requires
    marketing to get the word out about your new
    seminar. In the past all it required was a simple
    direct mail piece sent out by the post office. Now it
    requires social media, blogging, your website, the
    Internet, to name a few of the tools that you will be
    using to market your seminar. Can you affiliate with a
    professional association that might be willing to offer
    publicity about your seminar to its members? Can
    you gather a mail or e-mail list of members of an
    organization that might be interested in your topic?
    Do you know a blog or Internet site that would
    feature your seminar to its readers? You have
    produced the next great seminar, but you are
    wondering how to attract that room full of people
    who all will pay top dollar to attend.

4. Are these people willing to pay the fee you have
    selected for the seminar?

You need to find the exact magic price to charge for attending your seminar. What is that price that will attract the right number of people? Everyone has a price for attending a seminar beyond which it is too expensive for him or her. It will require your testing the water to see just how high you can go before you experience seminar attendee fall-off. Take a look at what the professional seminar companies are charging. Keep in mind the salary level of the audience you are trying to attract. You need to ask who is going to pay for their attendance at your seminar. Is it their employer who might have a training budget, or is it the prospect themselves taking it from their family budget? This question of "how much should I charge" is one of the most difficult ones you will face. You are trying to find that pricing "sweet spot." How do want the audience out there to see your seminar? Are you the "Wal Mart" of seminars or are you attempting to be the Nordstrom of seminars? Are you attempting to gather more audience members by offering a low fee or do you want a higher paid audience but less of them? You want to ask yourself exactly what value you are offering to those people attending your seminar. If you can state clearly the value you are offering, you can set the price to match that value. What is your seminar going to give to your attendee? Can you show this value?

5. Are similar seminars being offered and if so, are they in the same location where you are planning to offer yours?

Again, do not panic if similar seminars are being offered. This may simply indicate that you have a viable topic that lots of people need and are willing to pay to attend. Of course, if you do not find similar seminars to yours out there, it could indicate that your topic has passed its prime or it is of extremely limited interest. Spend time on the Internet to check out similar seminars and to see where they are being offered. Check the cost to attend these seminars and see if your seminar fits into this mix.

As you research your topic you may find that similar seminars are being offered in a nearby area. This may cause you concern since these seminars are only a few miles away from your planned one. The truth is that most people who attend seminars have no idea what is being offered just outside their living space. Community colleges offer the exact same seminars in the next town since people only find seminars by looking in their local college brochure. Many seminar companies do not consider offering the same seminar twenty miles a part and fail to realize that this is a whole new audience, completely unaware of the other seminar location. Even by offering the same seminar on a different night in the next town might interest a new group to attend.

It could be an advantage if your seminar is priced higher or lower than the others.

It is like going wine tasting. Many wines are priced so high that people desire them and will want to show them off to all their friends. Think Screaming Eagle at $850 a bottle or visiting Trader Joes and purchasing a bottle of two-buck chuck for only a few dollars. Both wines are drinkable but the value to the purchaser is very different. To many people an expensive seminar gives their ego a pleasant feeling and they love to mention their attendance to friends.

You need to research these questions before locking in on a seminar topic. Let's explore each of these to see how we might find the best answers. One critical issue is how to find those people who care about or need your topic. Consider where are you planning to hold your seminar and how large the population is in that area. Is it a bedroom community or a corporate location? Does this area fit well with the type of seminar you are offering? If your seminar is quite expensive, are you offering it in an area that can afford it? After you decide that the topic is needed and that people are willing to pay your fee, then you need to consider how to locate them.

Let me give you an example of a seminar that we offer for the executive directors of non-profit agencies. I have worked in this field in the past and realize that there are a multitude of topics that would interest this audience. These executive directors have many things on their plates. They are concerned about satisfying their board of directors, locating volunteers, helping their clients, and raising funds to operate the agency. This tells me there are a wide variety of topics that would interest them. My task is to find which of the topics are the most critical to them. Would it be raising money or finding volunteers? Would it be figuring out how to work with their board of directors or dealing with their own staff? These are important questions. How do you find these answers? Where do you start?

You might start by locating the key publications in the non-profit field. These are the critical books, web sites, TED talks, social media, interviews, etc. You are looking for those key references to help you understand the audience and their needs. This research might be something that has changed in the past few years or it could be something that will be changing in the near future. Your question is what does your audience want to understand or be able to do following their attendance at your seminar.

You may want to conduct a needs assessment of your potential audience to find out how much knowledge they already have on your subject. You don't want to be seen as talking down to them by presenting something that they already have in their knowledge bank. You also do not want to go over their heads with your content.

It is critical that you present your topic at the right level based on your audience experience and prior learning.

These five questions suggest that you think of your seminar as a business. This means that you focus your attention on three critical things, your topic, your audience, and your budget. All three are critical to attracting the right attendees to your seminar. The topic will interest or not interest people. The topics will either attract them or they will ignore it. You need to offer something a large enough audience will sign up to attend. And you must have a large enough budget to allow you to market the seminar to enough people in your seminar location. Your budget also will allow you to select a facility large enough to host the size of audience that will bring you the income you desire. Nothing is more disheartening that having to turn people down because you have selected a too small seminar site.

Thinking About Your Seminar

I guess the best question is where should you start? You want to offer a seminar, but are not completely sure what topic to offer. You know what you think would be a good topic, but you're not sure that anyone will sign up for it. I suggest that there are very few bad seminar topics; there is only bad seminar marketing.

The fact that you are passionate about a topic tells me there are dozens of people out there that are also interested in that topic. Sometimes the more specific the subject the more interest you can generate in your audience. Something that is too broad may not grab your audience's attention. Something like *How to Make Money* will attract a very small audience while *How to Make Money as a Home-based Caterer* might fill the room. Your task is to fine-tune your topic to make your seminar more specific and alluring to your prospects.

You have seminar ideas right now, but may not be sure how to fine-tune them. I suggest that you start by visiting your local bookstore and see how many books are available on your topic. Generally, the more books, the better a seminar topic. It may indicate that there is a strong interest in that topic. But do not assume that because there are only a limited number of books that it may not be a strong and salable topic. Books are only printed for a large audience, but you might have that topic a small group would be willing to attend. At times a small group may want that seminar so badly that they will even pay a higher fee to attend. There may only be a few books on *How to build a WordPress Blog*, but there might be dozens of people ready to start on that project. They may want an opportunity to attend a seminar and gather one-on-one help from the instructor.

Your task is to give your audience information that will get them started.

You need to answer the question -what will they take with them when they leave your seminar? Can they apply that knowledge right away? That is your goal. One of the seminars I present is *How to Make Money as a Meeting Planner.* To be successful as a meeting planner, there are more than a dozen items you need to know. It is my job to present each of these items in enough detail to allow my audience to become knowledgeable about them. I do not expect that they will walk out of my seminar and apply for a job as a professional meeting planner. But I have given them a basic level of knowledge to start them learning more in each of the areas of meeting planning and hopefully be able to apply as an intern with a meeting planner.

Start Your Research

Once you decide on the topic for your seminar, it is time to start your research. You have found at least ten books in your field and spent a few days on the Internet finding everything you can about your topic.

Make a list of your major topics and the sub-topics that you need to present. Think of these as chapters in a book. Don't worry about putting things in the correct order just yet. You will be doing a lot of "cutting and pasting" in the days ahead.

For my *How to Make Money as a Meeting Planner* seminar, I started by listing the functions of the sales and catering office. Then listed the various positions at a hotel that deal with events. This would include all food and beverage events. This would cover dealing with a variety of vendors, as well as understanding the laws relating to service for the physical challenged. Timing and schedules would require a session as well.

After you list the topics to be covered in the seminar, it would be time to talk with professionals in that field and see what they think you may have missed. They can help you decide just how much time each section will require in order for you to cover it in enough detail. At this point you will decide if you are developing a half-day, full day or a multiple day seminar. Just remember the longer the seminar, the more you will need to charge for attendance and maybe less people will attend due to this increased cost.

As you develop these sub-topics, start to add folders to your computer database and label each with the topic name. Remember when we did this with folders in a file cabinet? I use a computer program called Evernote for this purpose. Evernote makes it easy to remember the details from your research. You will be conducting research using the computer, cell phone, tablet, and Internet. As you find anything relevant to each segment, save it and add it to your Evernote file.

Don't try to flesh out each topic just yet. I find each seminar has a number of key sections. For a three-hour seminar, I usually have five sections each having about 30 minutes of content. In a full-day seminar you will still have five sections but each section would be one hour long, still leaving time for breaks, lunch and introductions.

In my *Care & Feeding of Volunteers* seminar, I break the five sections down to Understanding Volunteers, Motivation, Recruitment, Retention, and Recognition. In the three-hour seminar, each of these five topics would receive 30 minutes of seminar presentation. This concept allows you to visualize the seminar and it allows you to begin fleshing out the content. Remember that in any seminar content is king. People attend to get your well-planned content. Remember that adult learning theory tells us to never waste anyone's time.

They are paying to learn and they want knowledge to take home and apply after the seminar.

As I plan these five sections, I start thinking of them as individual modules. The seminar moves along module by module. You are developing five modules and each module will be 30 minutes long. Each module might be expanded and become a seminar all by itself. My *Care & Feeding of Volunteers* seminar could expand into a three-hour or even a full day seminar. For example, I could offer a full day seminar on *How to Recruit Volunteers*.

The value of building your seminar module by module is that you have a 30-minute talk available for your local chamber of commerce or service club. These talks are perfect marketing tools to get people fired up to register for your seminar. They are a teaser to wet their interest. I call these short talks lead generators. They generate leads that might produce other paid speaking engagements or seminar registrations. This module format will let you build a different presentation when a client calls and needs only a piece of your seminar. Many times I have had an association call and want a one-hour keynote presentation and I was able to pull it from one of the seminar modules.

Each module is designed to have a beginning, middle and ending segment.

Each module will have an opening, then move through a few major points and end with a summary. This allows each module to be a stand-alone presentation. This allows your audience to sense a feeling of completion building as you move through the day. If a participant needs to leave early, they will still attend a number of complete segments during their time with you. These modules allow you to build audio, video, print and online webinars with only minor revisions.

One of the keys to successful seminar design is to give your audience complete content in the shortest amount of time. Content is the most important item in your presentation. Clear and concise content will position your seminar as a reliable source of information. Your content will help establish you and your seminar as a credible authority source. It will drive conversations and engage your audience. The more valuable this content is, the more you become an expert and gain your participants trust.

Design your content to communicate in simple language, using the language of your attendees.

Avoid corporate-speak and buzzwords. You will need to follow the typical three W's of journalism; why, who, and what. Let's look at these three W's and how they apply to your seminar design.

First, Why are you creating this content? In other words, what are your goals? What do you hope to accomplish? This "why" must be featured in all of your marketing materials? It is the prime reason that anyone will take the seminar. The task of marketing is to convince your potential attendee to sign up for the seminar. Isn't "why" the first word most children learn? "Why Daddy, why?"

Second, who is your audience and what do they already know about your content? Is this a live audience or an on-line one? What are their problems and how can this seminar solve them? You carefully figure out exactly who will be in your audience. What are their age, gender, professional background, and career path? Why are they signing up for this seminar?

And Third, What action do you want your participants to take after they leave the seminar? Can your content help them be successful at your topic? Do you have testimonials from past attendees that will convince your prospects that you know what you are doing?

Let me say it again, keep the content practical and cover it in the shortest amount of time. The problem with so many university classes is they are structured to go for three hours a session, eighteen weeks, whether they need that much time or not. This is your seminar. You can produce a seminar to last only as long as it needs to be. Your trial runs will help you determine how much ground you can cover in exactly how much time.

Select the Most Effective Title

Let's drill down on our seminar planning. One critical item in seminar planning is to select the best title to attract our attendees. The seminar title is the lure to start attracting potential attendees. The title needs to be simple and self-explainable. Too many people try to be creative with their titles and completely miss the point.

The title of this book is *SeminarBiz* with a subtitle of *How to Make Money in the Seminar Business*. It is not *The Seminar Business*. Does the first attract more people? What is your goal in learning about the seminar business? Is it to find a business that gives you a good return on your investment? Do you want to know exactly how to produce a seminar that is successful and earns money? The title should hit the target audience right between their eyes with a goal in mind. Sometimes the audience is not even aware of their goal but your title might help them find it.

From a marketing standpoint nothing is more critical than selecting the best title for your seminar. The title should be selected based on your audience. It must be selected from their viewpoint. Assuming you are producing a seminar on the new laws relating to the real estate profession, you might title your seminar "New Laws in Real Estate." This title will tell your potential audience what you are planning to cover, but not why they should consider signing up for it. If you view your title from your audiences' perspective you might try "How New Laws Will Impact Your Sales Numbers." This might change your seminar from one of academic interest into something of personal interest. Sometimes you might use the words "How To" as in the title, *How To Make Money in Catering.* That might interest more people than simply a title of *Catering 101.*

Start by reviewing the Internet and Amazon for possible titles. Don't steal titles, just use the other titles are an idea base. For example, books on starting your own seminar business are *How to Make it Big in the Seminar Business, Start Your Own Seminar Production Business* and *The Complete Secrets to Seminar Success.* You can see how these book titles give you thoughts about how to get your seminar business underway. These titles talk about making it big, starting it up and what are the secrets. All of them are more effective that the typical college course title of Seminars 101.

People do not want to know everything; they simply want to know what the presenter thinks it will take to be successful.

The purpose of the title is to attract an audience to your seminar. This audience is important because they are the ones paying to attend. It is worth spending time to create an effective title. Sit down and think of keywords that describe what your seminar involves. What words describe your seminar outcome? What are the results you want to achieve by the end of your offering? A one-word title is very effective with a more complete sub-title filling in the details. A one-word title is challenging to write, but highly effective. Your title can set an expectation with your audience.

Search on Amazon.com for book titles in the same genre as your planned seminar. You might look at www.goodreads.com for a fun series of book titles to start your thinking. Which titles do you like? Which ones don't you like and why? Spend the time looking for effective titles and it will start your creative thinking process flowing. Look at business book titles like "Good To Great" or "Drive" or "Total Money Makeover." Look at www.findaseminar.com for a wide variety of seminar titles. Findaseminar.com gives you multiple ways to search for seminars, workshops, and conferences.

Try to come up with a dozen or so titles and then put your list away for a few days. When you come back to it you will be surprised which ones feel best. The correct title promises your attendee a benefit. It is easy to remember, and sets your seminar apart from all the others. It also creates a brand for you and your seminar. Short titles are effective and long titles are too easy to forget or they may be confusing. Short titles are far more likely to be remembered.

Titles that are effective might use numbers or letters such as *7 Keys to a Successful Marriage* or *Five steps to a Great Romance.* People all think they know some of the keys to a successful marriage, but do they know all seven? Some books use higher numbers such as *1001 Ways to Market Your Books.* The Dummy concept has been very effective, such as *Blogging for Dummies or iPhone for Dummies.*

A Few Legal Thoughts

You cannot use the Dummy title since is protected by trademark. A trademark is a brand name. A trademark includes any word, name, symbol, device, or any combination, used or intended to identify and distinguish the goods/services of one seller or provider from those of others, and to indicate the source of the goods/services. You can register your trademark, but is not required. But federal registration has several advantages, including a notice to the public of the registrant's claim of ownership of the mark, a legal presumption of ownership nationwide, and the exclusive right to use the mark on or in connection with the goods or services set forth in the registration. Your brand is your seminar's most important asset. Protect it.

Registering a trademark with the U.S. Patent and Trademark Office ("USPTO") gives you or your business the exclusive rights to use the name, brand or logo in question in the United States. Likewise, registration in other countries protects your trademark in those jurisdictions. If you wish to trademark your seminar title you need to put a symbol in small print following the title. If you do not register the trademark you wish to protect, just add TM after the title. When you have contacted the United States Patent and Trademark Office (USPTO) and paid a fee to register your trademark then you can add the symbol ® on your title. Both serve to prevent another person from using that title for a seminar. But when in doubt contact a trademark attorney as this book is not able to give legal advice.

Many people confuse a trademark with copyright. You want to place a copyright notice on your printed materials. A copyright protects works of authorship, such as writings, music, and works of art that have been tangibly expressed. Copyright protection does not extend to any idea, system, method, device, name, or title. For information on copyrights, go to www. Copyright.gov (a division of the Library of Congress) for information and online registration forms. While copyright registration is not required, registration is recommended for a number of reasons. Many choose to register their works because they wish to have the facts of their copyright on the public record and have a certificate of registration. Registered works may be eligible for statutory damages and attorney's fees in successful litigation. Finally, if registration occurs within 5 years of publication, it is considered *prima facie* evidence in a court of law. In either case, you should place the proper copyright notice © on the inside front page of your publication. This is to alert anyone that you have requested copyright protection for your published work.

Back to titles and away from all this legal talk. Many community colleges do a poor job of selecting appropriate titles for their offerings simply because they assume that academic titles will bring in the right audience. An example is *Small Business Basics* or *Effective Delegation.* College community education programs print a seminar brochure each season and send it out to their mailing list, which includes thousands of residents in their community. This is in many ways considered junk mail to most residents. Junk only because any mail coming in to your mailbox that does not interest you is not of value to you.

Unless people take the time to review the college catalog or they are searching for a specific course, it has limited value. It does not jump out of the mailbox and say, "read me." They may have written effective copy and developed a strong title but unless people pick it up and read it, they will miss the offering. If you work with a college and they agree to offer your seminar you will need to help market your class. The college has much to offer and they are good at furnishing a seminar room at no cost. Their weakness is generally marketing expertise. They depend on one bulk mailing for each semester. Their catalog will list a wide variety of over 100 classes. The chance of someone finding your class is limited due to the small amount of copy they can devote in their catalog to each offering. They offer publicity for your seminar and as long as you help to get the word out it is a worthwhile connection for you, particularly as you start in this business.

Even with a community college sponsor helping to offer your class, you will need a budget for marketing your seminar. You are enhancing the marketing the college does to insure that you obtain a large enough number of attendees in your room. This marketing that you do will include publicity in the local newspapers and features on the local television stations promoting your seminar.

The local media is generally hungry to promote interesting courses that the college offers. They will be very interested in interviewing you about the class, but unless you make the first contract, it might not happen. Even though the media will find your class worth promoting, they do not have the staff to search out every local seminar. It is your task to alert the media of the value that your seminar offers. The other advantage of using a community college to sponsor your seminar is that the media considers their offerings a public service. With your own seminar offering without a college sponsor they will expect you to buy advertising space to help gain visibility.

If you roll out your seminar without college sponsorship, you will be covering all marketing expenses. All publicity and travel expenses will be out of your own pocket. It is a good idea to have a local college sponsor your seminar for at least a year while you iron out the details and starts to collect a little income for your "roll-out" fund. The amount you are earning from the college will be limited, but this is an excellent way to test your seminar viability.

How Much Should You Charge?

Since we are talking about income from your seminar, it might be a good place to discuss exactly how much to charge for your seminar. Certainly you must consider all the costs involved in producing the seminar and how you can hold these costs to a minimum amount. The profit is impacted by how much you will charge each person attending. This is determined by how much each seminar costs to operate. Your seminar fee depends on two things. First what is the true value of this seminar to your attendees? Just how much is your content worth to them? Are you offering something that is extremely hard to find? How much time will you be saving them by attending your event? The more value your seminar holds for the attendee, the higher the price you can ask. Since a large percentage of your income might be coming from back-of-the-room sales and from future consulting, you want to consider that in setting your fee.

You need to price your seminar high enough to convince your attendee that it has value, but not so high that it excludes people who might be customers.

Some folks go so far with there pricing philosophy that they offer the seminar for free to attempt to entice future customers. It may be a financial planner who wants customers for his firm. He might feel the seminar will build credibility with people and that this could lead to a new client base. One problem with offering a free seminar is that a free seminar generally has no value to many people, and in fact might scare some people away from enrolling. They may correctly assume that a free seminar is an opportunity for the presenter to attempt to sell them something. Free seminars may cause your prospects to devalue what you have to offer. They might think that it will have limited value. Otherwise why would you give it away for free?

You are much better off pricing your seminar at a fair price and then offer them the opportunity to work with you in the future. You could offer them a "professional discount" or even refund some or the entire seminar fee, if they work with you at a later date. The other problem with a free seminar is that you are not allowing your attendees to have any "skin in the game." They are more likely to fail to show up for a free seminar, than if they have invested dollars to attend it. We all get those mailings offering a free dinner and seminar if we would sign up for this event. Most of us just put that flyer in the trash can because we feel it is a high-pressure sales gimmick. You do not want your seminar to be in that category.

The seminar price is critical for attracting the right audience into your seminar.

If you are planning to sell back-of-the-room products you need to have a proper fee for enrollment to insure that you have people who can afford your products. If your price for the seminar too high, it might limit your audience numbers and not give you enough people to purchase your products. It is always a good idea to price check similar seminars. Just "Google" your topic with the word "seminar" and see what shows up. It is also smart to test your price to see how it affects both attendance and product sales. You could offer a seminar at one fee and another at a higher fee and see if it makes any difference with registration. If you get the same number or even a larger enrollment with a higher fee it will tell you what you need to know. What it will tell you is go with the higher fee. To some people the higher fee indicates a higher quality seminar.

Consider your policy on no-shows, cancellations, or even people asking to change seminar dates. If your attendee simply decides to cancel the seminar, what is your policy? Do you allow them to get a full refund? Does it make any difference how far ahead of the seminar they request this refund? *Fred Pryor Seminars* allows you to send a substitute from your organization or to transfer your registration fee to another seminar of your choice that is scheduled within 12 months of the original seminar date. Many seminar firms put a statement in their brochure stating that within so many days the attendee can receive a refund minus a cancellation fee. Most firms will state that if you fail to show up for a seminar you lose your entire fee. Here is an example of a cancellation policy from a major seminar provider:

Cancellation Policy: If you cancel 10 days or less from the event date your full tuition will be forfeited, but you may apply it to future seminars within one year of your first scheduled seminar. If you cancel more than 10 days prior to the event date then a $95 fee will be retained to cover administrative costs.

Here is another cancellation policy from a different provider:

Notification of your cancellation must be in writing. Cancellations received up to the day prior to the program are subject to a US$250 cancellation charge. No refunds are given once the program has begun. Registrants who fail to attend a program are not entitled to a refund.

You may want to consider offering a discount for early registration. Registrations for seminars tend to come in three stages, one-third will sign-up early if they are offered a discount. Another third will sign up midway in the cycle and they may be the ones who need to convince their boss or spouse of the seminar value. Then, the last third will sign up the week before the seminar or they just show up at the door the day of the seminar.

Many seminar firms offer an "early bird" registration fee if you sign up for the seminar before a certain date. It can increase your advance registration and bring you a higher level of confidence that your seminar is attracting as you hoped it would. Here is a sample of early bird registration for a seminar.

Early Bird Registration for this Seminar closes this Friday, September 2 at 11:59 pm (Pacific Standard Time) If you have not already done so, please click here to register.

You might consider a lower fee if a group of three or more plan to attend the same seminar on the same day. This discount might be 10% or more on each registration. The idea behind this discount is to interest businesses to send a group to gather your training all at one time. It is an incentive to the company paying to send employees for training and it saves them a few dollars at the same time. Here is a sample of a group discount statement from a business seminar firm brochure:

We offer group discounts for multiple participants from the same company at any single seminar location.

Send 2 participants: Each receives a 5% tuition discount

Send 3-5 participants: Each receives a 10% tuition discount

Send 6 or more participants: Each receives a 15% tuition discount

Many companies will consider this a strong incentive to send more people to your seminar and it certainly increases your bottom line.

As you consider the amount to charge each seminar participant, think about the numbers. Should you price your seminar at $100 or $99? It is interesting that many people see $99 as less than $100. Randy Gage, a well-known speaker who talks on prosperity has an interesting thought about pricing anything. Randy uses sevens to end everything on his product list. His tapes are $197 and his videos are $347. He feels that ending in a seven is much more friendly and effective than ending in a nine. I follow his advice and always priced my seminars at $177 for a one-day seminar and $97 for a half-day seminar.

To compute the budget, let's look at your costs. The best way to figure out how much to charge for your seminar is to find out how much each seminar will cost you. Marketing costs will vary by the number of attendees you wish to attract. If you plan to send out both print and digital announcements for your seminar and you anticipate getting one percent of that mailing to register, then you can estimate the cost of each attendee. If you send out 1,000 seminar flyers, you can plan to have ten people sitting in your seminar. A capture ratio of one-half to one percent of your mailing is fairly accurate. This is true with both print and digital mailings. If each mailing piece costs fifty cents each, then your total mailing cost for 1,000 pieces is $500. If you charge $97 to register for your seminar, your ten attendees would bring in $970. This is a rough way to figure your marketing costs, but it helps to think of your numbers like this. This would assume that you are printing a flyer and paying for rented names and labels.

If you have been collecting your own e-mail addresses and plan to use digital e-mail marketing, then your costs will be lower. Using U.S. postage is both effective and expensive since you must design and print a brochure and then direct mail it via the U.S. Postal service. Once you design your seminar brochure and have it printed, you need to rent a mailing list and have the labels printed and affixed those labels to your brochure. You can use a mailing service do this, but that will increase your costs.

Your Seminar Day

You are the expert for the day! You are the person on the stage with all the answers. They have paid good money to hear what you have to say. You must have the answers they want or at least be willing to find the answers for them. Give them the opportunity to meet with you during all the breaks and plan to stay around after the seminar to answer questions.

These are the people who will recommend your seminar, attend the next one, and purchase your books, tapes and other materials. If you convince them that you are the person with the answers, they may want your consulting knowledge for a fee at a later date. Be sure to gather complete information on every participant. This is so that you can market learning opportunities to them. Be sure to mention during the seminar that you are available if they have any questions. Give them your business card. Be sure your card has your cell phone number and website on it. You should insure that every handout has all of this contact information on it.

Be sure that your material is 100% up-to-date. Let your audience know they should be careful with books they find in the marketplace, as they may be out of date. You are letting them know that you are the person for them to recommend as an expert in this content area. Plan to continually revise everything so that it reflects current information.

Your Opinion Counts!

Your attendees expect that you will have opinions and that you will clearly express them.

They are paying money to attend your seminar and they expect your personal opinion on everything. It is smart to start the seminar by telling your audience that you will be sharing your opinions. Try not to put down competitors, but simply let the audience know what products you use and why you use them. If you endorse products, be sure to let them know if you have any financial agreement with these companies or individuals.

Let them know that you will be discussing ideas and products that you have found useful in your professional life. Give them the specific web sites and tools that you use and tell they why you have selected them. This is part of the value of attending your seminar as opposed to reading a book on this subject. They have an opportunity to ask you just about anything.

The All-important Questions and Answers

Consider having question and answer opportunities during the entire seminar rather than having your audience hold questions until the end of the day. When people have a question, it is difficult for them to wait until later. They will forget the question or might even be upset with you for not allowing their question to be asked at that time. Let them know that they can ask questions at anytime during the seminar. Be friendly but do not allow any individual to too take over the seminar with multiple questions. This allows them to take advantage of everyone's seminar time.

The value of Q & A is that an audience member may have the best answer to a question or recommendation to a supplier. Let your audience answer each other's questions with recommendations from their personal experiences. They may have more experience in certain areas of the seminar than you do.

Get in the habit of repeating a question before you answer it. You have the microphone and they may not be able to hear the question. A guest in the audience may have hearing issues and they will appreciate your repeating it. It is a good idea to have one of your staff with a microphone visit the person asking the question. But never allow that person to take the microphone away from your staff member. That can lead to a delay as that person is now in control of your seminar and might end up wasting everyone's time.

Morning, Afternoon or Evening?

You can present your seminar in the morning, afternoon or evening, which is best? Each one has advantages and disadvantages. For many people starting early in the morning is best. They are wide-awake and very alert. But you need to consider traffic flow and parking issues and thereby build in a little extra time after your announced start time before you actually begin your seminar. Tell people that the seminar starts with registration and coffee at 8:30 a.m. and that the seminar will start at 9:00 a.m. This will give everyone an opportunity to get caught in traffic, find a parking spot and still arrive on time. But do not delay beyond your stated start time or you will disturb those who showed up right on time as you requested.

If you hold an afternoon seminar, it is good to begin with registration at 1 p.m. and start the seminar at

1:30 p.m. This will allow your people to grab lunch on the way to the seminar. You will have to project more energy into your afternoon session since people have already worked half their day and just had lunch.

You may want to start your evening seminar at 6:30 p.m. with registration and begin the seminar at 7 p.m. An evening seminar may be even more difficult with stomachs full of dinner and maybe a glass of wine. Be sure to move around more, call everyone by name and maybe just splash them with water. (Just kidding).

Your Seminar Presentation Design

Many seminar designers will start with PowerPoint or Keynote and lay out the content in slide form. This is helpful because it allows you to see the layout visually and it is easy to make content changes. But be careful with PowerPoint. Many of you have heard of *Death by PowerPoint*. Many seminars are little more than three-hour slide shows. You may have taken a nap during many of those seminars.

The presenter probably flashed rapid and (if it was PowerPoint) colorful sequences of text and tables and charts. Sometimes they asked questions of the audience and either had no response or a response from the same two or three people over and over again. If the participants didn't have a workbook with copies of the slides in front of them, they would frantically take notes in a futile effort to keep up with the hundreds of slides. If they did get a printed copy of the slides, they probably decided that they could just as easily view the slides at a more convenient time and they went on their smart phone checking today's e-mail. Too often the presenter reads the slide bullets to the audience. This makes everyone wonder why the presenter did not just hand out a copy of the slides and let them goes home. I guess you feel my negative reaction to most PowerPoint use during seminars.

If you follow my suggestions on the use of PowerPoint, you are going to get mixed reviews from many of your friends. Many people use PowerPoint because they feel that it's the proper way to conduct a seminar. In Eric Bergman's book *Death By PowerPoint* he tells us that PowerPoint is not the problem. He says, "PowerPoint is not flawed. The program simply has become a victim of its own success."

The issue is that many people put way too much text on each slide.

The question is whether all that text is necessary in the first place. The problem is the belief that slides are needed at all. Bergman tells it best when he says,

"That's the way it's done, and that's the way it's always been done." I think most audiences will tell you that they have been overdosed on slides during most presentations.

The problem with all that text on the screen is that people cannot read and listen at the same time. Have you even been given a newspaper to read and your friend continues to talk at the same time you are attempting to read. It is next to impossible to read and listen to your friend at the same time.

You have seen many presentations using PowerPoint, but it is rare to find an outstanding one. I can suggest two books to give you simple design principles. They are *Presentation zen Design* by Garr Reynolds and *Presentation Secrets* by Alexei Kapterev. Both books give us a strong approach to designing and delivering successful and provocative presentations. Garr says, "every design has a central concept or message and anything that leads to confusion or distracts from your intended message is considered noise." Too many a series of slides with plenty of charts and text means that you are serious about your work. Many people feel that if the slides look complicated, they must be good. Garr Reynolds says it well by stating "Nobody can do a good presentation with slide after slide of bullet points." He says that bullet point's work well when used sparingly in documents to help readers scan content or summarize key points. But in a seminar, your audience will tire quickly if you show slide after slide of bulleted lists. Bullet points should be used rarely and only when required to clearly make the message stronger.

Use Attention Organizers

Rather than using bullet points, build attention organizers into you seminar presentations. You might wonder, what are attention organizers? It is anytime someone says to you " you better make a note of this." This alerts you that something important is coming next. If you say "the three most important ways to..." it will wake your audience up. They will wonder if they know all three ways. If the teacher tells the class "this will be on the exam," you can bet everyone picks up their pencil and starts taking notes. These are attention organizers and they help direct attention to key points in the presentation. Be careful not to overdo this process or you will lose the value of your attention organizers.

It is a good idea to use visual support such as photographs, drawings, handouts, brochures, and actual products that you can pass around the room during the seminar. People love things they can hold and touch. If you are talking about a police rap sheet during a risk management seminar, why not pass a physical rap sheet around so people can touch it. Even if you are projecting one on the screen, it is helpful to pass copies around the room so people can actually hold one. If the group were fairly large you would need a number of copies to avoid them taking too much time traveling around the room.

Case Studies and War Stories

Building *case studies* or *war stories* into your presentation is a very good way to create concrete examples in the minds of your audience. These bring the "real world" into the seminar room. These case studies and war stories are best when they belong to the presenter. *Case studies* are generally stories from business schools that illustrate specific examples. Case studies are often used during breakout sessions where a small group of participants discuss the case and attempt to understand the point of the story. A *war story* is a real-life experience from the presenter that gives an example from their life experience. A war story adds color to the topic by having the presenter talk about something that actually happened. Let me give you an example of one of my war stories from a seminar that I present on customer service.

We were conducting a seminar last year in a Hyatt hotel in Chicago when I noticed all of the employees wearing a big round badge on their jackets that stated 10 & 5. I was curious about the badge and I had to find out what the 10 & 5 meant. So when we entered an elevator with one of the staff I asked him what the 10 & 5 badges were all about. He said he was so embarrassed, but that everyone had to wear the badges because they were caught not following the Hyatt 10 & 5 rule. I asked, what is that rule? He said that at any Hyatt hotel all staff must smile at a guest ten feet from them and as they get closer, 5 feet from the guest they must always say Good Morning or Good Evening. They were caught not doing it and now they have to wear that badge for an entire month and all their guests are asking about the 10 & 5 badge.

This is an example of a war story that gives the participants a chance to think about a real customer service experience. I give the story orally and we discuss how this experience improved Hyatt customer service. This it is a good opportunity to ask if any of the attendees have a similar story that can help to illustrate customer service.

Checklists and Resource Lists

Everyone attending a seminar enjoys receiving checklists and resource lists. They might be included in the seminar workbook or might be distributed during the seminar as the presenter is discussing them. Checklists are a step-by-step guide to insuring a process is followed correctly. A checklist is a type of informational aid used to ensure consistency and completeness in carrying out a task. It is a sort of "to do" list. This is a list with small checkboxes down the left side of the page.

The resource list will give them additional tools to use in the future. It might contain books, tools, and places where you can find needed materials. Make this resource list a very personal listing of items. This makes it more very valuable. This should be items that you use and highly recommend. It might be items that you gain income from recommending or not. Let your participants know that when they purchase these items you gain income. Again, you should disclose any connections that you have with any service or product that you recommend.

Start Strong and End Strong

Design your seminar to start strong and end strong. Plan your opening lines and practice them multiple times. Do not memorize your entire presentation because if you do, you might lose your thoughts as soon as someone asks you a question. It is important to know your opening and closing lines cold. All presenters are nervous when they start a seminar. That is just nervous energy and is very helpful to get you started on the right foot. It has been said that most audiences only give you about four minutes before they start tuning you out if you are not interesting. Your opening is intended to get the audience on your side. Your opening needs to be your strong start. Even though you have notes for your entire presentation, the opening should be well planned and rehearsed.

Written notes help you keep the flow and sequence of your presentation. Use computer-typed notes using an easy to read typeface of at least 18-point type. Print your notes with a maximum of white space and on heavier card stock. This heavier paper will allow you to slide your notes on the table. Do not staple them together as they will make noise and they are hard to handle. Do not use the standard classroom 3 x 5 cards because you may drop them at some point during your seminar.

Depending on the number of people in your room, you might allow your participants to introduce themselves. You could walk around with a microphone to allow everyone in the room to hear the introductions. The value of this is to provide your guests with that important networking opportunity which occurs during breaks. Your attendees are looking to meet people from the same line of work or who live in the same neighborhood. I suggest to my audience that they give their first name, employer name, and the city where they live or work. This has nothing to do with privacy issues. It's simply that most people can only remember someone's first name under those conditions. Giving your first name also matches the name badges that all your guests are wearing as well.

This is a nice way to start that very important networking phase and it only takes a few minutes of their valuable seminar time. If you have a smaller group, maybe up to 50 people, you might want to have tent cards on their tables with their first names on them. If you use tent cards be sure to put their names on both sides so that people sitting behind them can see their names as well. Print the cards with large type (at least 144 point type) so that they can be legible from a distance.

Seminar Room Layout

I prefer a *Classroom Style* room layout that uses both tables and chairs. The seats are in rows facing the stage area. The tables allow your attendees to write their notes. It is difficult to take notes in a theater style without tables.

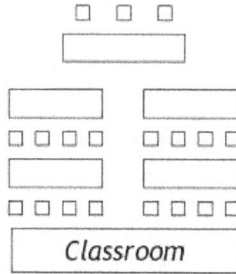

Classroom

Be sure to tell the hotel catering staff that you want tables and chairs, not just chairs. You want long, narrow tables placed in rows with chairs on one side facing the stage. Hotels do not charge extra for the tables. It is best to ask for the 24 inch wide by 8-foot long tables. Never allow chairs on both sides of the table or half your audience will be facing backward and will have to turn around to see the stage. You will need at least 2 feet of space per person at each table. The minimum space between tables should be 3 feet and if possible, even 3 ½ feet.

It is a good idea to have the tables angled toward the center of the room. This is called *Chevron style.*

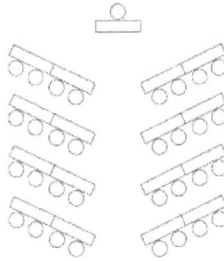

This classroom set-up allows the presenter to see all participants and the tables give your attendees space for note taking and to enjoy their cup of coffee and water. This chevron style also allows each participant to have a better view of the presenter and the stage.

If you have a small group, maybe limited to no more than 24 people, you might consider a U-shape set-up. This is when the tables are placed in a "U" shape.

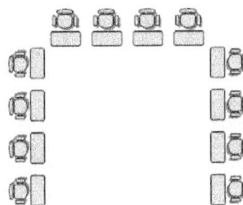

Chairs should be on the outside of the "U" allowing each person to face the speaker. Figure at least 2 feet of space per person. Have the hotel skirt the inside of the "U" since your attendees are only sitting on the outside. The opening of the "U" faces the stage and allows the presenter to walk into the audience.

Your Close

Remember that in sales you were told that if you do not ask, you will not get the sale. Your close should recap what you have been presenting. It's like that statement we all heard in high school speech class. "Tell them what you are going to tell them, tell them, and then tell them what you told them." This is actually good advice.

Your closing is your personal call for action. It should be something that people are thinking about as they walk to their cars. It should recap the whole day in a few strong sentences. When someone asks one of your attendees what they thought of the seminar they will probably repeat your closing statements. This closing statement is, along with your opening, is the most important part of your seminar.

Prepare this strong closing for your seminar because it is the last few words that everyone remembers.

What are Your Options for Sponsorship?

When you start seminar planning you have a few options to consider. First, you need to locate a strong topic that people are willing to pay for. Second, you design the content and third, you start to market the seminar. This means that you are in charge of everything. You do it all yourself or you hire a little outside assistance. This is a fun but risky way to start because you are underwriting all the cost. If you offer the seminar and nobody shows up, you have spent a fair amount of your own money and it is all gone. You have spent your budget on the room, the coffee, and the promotion.

Maybe a better way to start would be to find a sponsor. Sponsors are people or organizations that would see value in having their name attached to your event. There are a number of potential sponsors available for your seminar. One of the best is your local community college. Community colleges offer a number of continuing education classes on a wide variety of topics. Your topic might be one they would consider offering.

Your topic must be one that the college feels would fit their demographics. These courses are generally, but not always non-credit courses. They are for adults that want to increase their personal learning in specific areas. It might be a business or a personal interest course. Most will offer a variety of classes aimed at adults. These classes will generally be three-hour, half-day or full day classes offered in the evening and on weekends. They might include cooking classes, health and wellness classes or business classes to name a few categories.

One class that is offered through Sierra College in Roseville California is "Present Like a Pro." It is a class that teaches presentation skills. It meets one time for three hours and costs $56 to attend. The college supplies the publicity and marketing for the class and the instructor prepares the content and shows up on the scheduled day and presents the class.

For presenting the class, the instructor is paid a few hundred dollars or more depending on your agreement with the college. The value of this sponsorship is that the college covers all the costs of filling the room with students. Depending on the popularity of your offering, you will have a large number of attendees or possibly a very small number. If the number is too small, the college may decide to cancel the class.

You would put together a proposal to submit your topic to the college to see if they have any interest in it. The department offering these classes for adults might go by a variety of names, such as community education, continuing education or extension. The colleges have a proposal form generally on-line where you outline your topic and your personal background. The college staff will review your topic and decide if it has merit for their program. If they have a similar class already in their catalog, they will decide which class has more potential for registration. They will review your professional background in this subject area and see if it fits into their program. You do not have to have a college degree. Your professional background might be the reason you are selected to teach the course.

Colleges are attempting to offer a service to their community with these classes. But they need to earn enough income from the classes to keep their program alive and well. You do not have to be a credentialed teacher to teach a non-credit class at a college. You are not teaching in their degree program. They simply want an instructor who has the experience to teach this class.

Once the college decides that your offering might draw a large enough group of students, it will ask you about the possible dates for the class. After a date is set, they will discuss your fee to teach the class. At that point you will review the fee they offer and see if you are in agreement with their fee schedule. Many times they will offer a percentage of the class fee to be shared with the instructor. It might be 60% of the class fee going to the college and 40% going to the instructor.

I attempt to negotiate a 50% split with the college. That means that if they charge each attendee $50 for the course, then we both earn $25. If the class registers 40 students, then both the college and the instructor earn $1000 each.

The college usually has a minimum number of students registered before the class can be offered.

It might be as low as ten students. You might decide your minimum number of students as you are giving your time for a small amount of income, if the numbers are too small.

Starting your seminar business using other people's money (OPM) can be an excellent way to help your start-up seminar business. For this reason your connection with a community college might be worthwhile. Most larger communities have a community college and the majority of them hold continuing education classes as a service to their adult community. If you offer one to three classes at each college every semester, you will have an strong opportunity to grow your seminar business. The nice thing is that you are growing your business using their money and location. Being associated with a college will give your seminar a strong level of credibility and will give you positive relationships in the community.

How do you start your seminar business with community colleges?

First, locate a list of all your local Community Colleges. For example, in California there are 112 community colleges. Next collect all of the community college bulletins. This is simple because each college has their course catalog on-line. Reviewing each college catalog, see if that campus offers a similar course to yours, If not, then send an e-mail to the college's community education director. This e-mail will include a description of your seminar.

My first offerings were seminars focused on attracting non-profit directors of volunteer programs. This included paid or volunteer staff working for any governmental, educational, church, or non-profit group. I had already produced *The Care & Feeding of Volunteers* seminar. The seminar was three hours long. The first college was planning to charge a reasonable $49 for the class and they agreed to split that fee with me 50/50. So I would earn $24.50 for each person signing up for a class. If the average enrollment were 30 students per class that would give the college and the instructor $735 income each per class. You could offer two different classes on the same day, one in the morning and another in the afternoon. Students could sign up for one or both classes. Many of the attendees will sign for both classes and therefore the daily income for the college and myself would $1470 each. If more people than 30 sign up, it would give both of us a larger paycheck. After your positive experience at this first college, you could contact other colleges to offer the same classes in other locations.

Since there are a large number of community colleges it presents a wonderful opportunity. If you offer a class and it does not reach the minimum number, then the college simply cancels the class with no real loss to anyone. You will know about this cancellation long before you travel to the college. The cancellation usually takes place at least two weeks before the class date. Since most classes will enroll more than the minimum number of attendees, you can bring in a fair amount of income offering your seminars just two days a week. True, you have travel, lodging and meals to cover, but since you are driving and staying in budget hotels it can work out to your benefit.

Universities also offer these types of classes and generally offer full-day classes on the weekends and charge a higher fee, so it is better for you as well. The key to using community colleges and universities is the advantage of not using your money to offer these seminars. You have no risk of losing money on these seminars. This is a good example of using other people's money (OPM). It is a viable relationship for both you and the college.

You might continue this relationship with the colleges for a few years and bank the income from these seminars. Then use this income as marketing money for the first season of your own seminars.

How Do You Fill Your Seminar Room?

The greatest seminar has no value if the room is empty! Remember it is the marketing that fills up your seminar room. No marketing, no attendees. People need to find out about your seminar before they will spend money to attend it. When your seminar flyer arrives in someone's mailbox, either their U.S. Post Office mailbox or their e-mail box, they might consider it junk mail. Even if they look at it, they might not have any interest in your seminar.

One of the fears of the beginning seminar organizer is that you will spend time building a seminar, offering it to the public and having nobody show up. Yes, this could happen. In fact, it has happened to me. I remember one time in Ohio when I offered a seminar and two people arrived. What did I do? I presented the seminar and all three of us enjoyed it. What an intimate experience. But something was very wrong with the marketing for that event. There may have been any number of things that went wrong. It might have been the wrong topic, the wrong location, the wrong time of the year. But what I did was to sit down and analyze the event. In my case the marketing was wrong. I was offering the seminar too close to a major holiday.

When I started planning my seminar using my own marketing dollars, I had to be very selective in just who I targeted. I used standard industrial classification (SIC) codes and spent hours, maybe really days, searching for every possible SIC code that might represent an attendee. Standard Industrial Classification (SIC) codes are four digit numerical codes assigned by the U.S. government to business establishments to identify the primary business of the establishment. The classification was developed to facilitate the collection, presentation and analysis of data; and to promote uniformity and comparability in the presentation of statistical data collected by various agencies of the federal

112

government, state agencies and private organizations. The classification covers all economic activities.

The SIC system arrays the economy into 11 divisions, that are divided into 83 2-digit major groups, that are further subdivided into 416 3-digit industry groups, and finally disaggregated into 1,005 4-digit industries.

What is a Primary SIC code?

Each and every company will have a primary SIC code. This number indicates a company's primary line of business. What determines a company's primary SIC code is the code definition that generates the highest revenue for that company at a specific location in the past year. The first two digits of the code identify the major industry group, the third digit identifies the industry group and the fourth digit identifies the industry. For example SIC 81 represents legal services and SIC 8111 represents establishments headed by members of the bar and are primarily engaged in offering legal advice or services. SIC 81110205 represents attorneys in criminal law.

Your marketing campaign is nothing without your mailing list -- literally. Your mailing list needs to be in tip-top shape to make your campaign as effective as possible. But how do you go about doing this?

To increase your response rate, you need to spend extra time and attention picking the *right* mailing list. When you're new to direct marketing, it's tempting to try to cut costs by any means necessary. Sometimes, a mailing list broker can seem like an unnecessary expense. You might be thinking, "I'll just find the lists on my own."

The success or failure of any direct mail marketing effort completely hinges on the quality of the mailing list.

Alan Sharpe, President of Sharpe Copy, a business to business (B2B) direct mail agency tells us, "Last time I checked, there was 25,000 direct mail response lists and 50,000 compiled lists currently on the market." Sharpe shares that among all of these lists, "you'll find hundreds that work for your product or service but you likely won't find them because locating the best names for your mailing is complicated and best left to an experienced list broker." A list broker is a specialist who researches and recommends lists for you, and manages all the paperwork and other details of acquiring the list.

I knew that my seminar on volunteer management would include a variety of law enforcement agencies. To search for these I reviewed the SIC code for law enforcement and realized that each division has a unique code. I knew that government establishments primarily engaged in law enforcement, traffic safety, police and other activities related to the enforcement of the law and preservation of order. Government establishments primarily engaged in prosecution are classified in Industry 9222.

As I searched SIC codes for police protection, I found the following codes;

922101   Federal Government Police

922102   State Government Police

922103   Sheriff

922104   Police Departments

922106   Bailiffs

I noticed that sheriff's departments were different from police departments that were different from federal law enforcement agencies. SIC codes allow

116

you to select the exact agencies you want to target
with your seminar mailing.

You do not purchase mailing labels; you rent them
from a mailing list broker. They locate the owner of
the lists and allow you to rent the lists for a one-time
use. These lists are usually seeded which meant the
owner of the list might add decoy names to the list
that is mailed right back to the company that rented
the list to you. So if you cheat by copying the list and
then do a second mailing without paying a second
time, they will catch you and a new bill will arrive in
the mail.

These mailing lists, either street addresses or e-mail
lists generally give you about a ½ to 1 percent return.
That sounds awful, but it is really okay. You mail 100
pieces to gather one attendee. Remember the cost of
your mailing is not just the rental of the list, but must
include the printing of labels, the printing of the
flyer, and the cost of affixing the label to the
brochure. You might want to sit on your floor
attaching the sticky labels to the flyers and then take

them to the post office. But once the size of the mailing started to reach the thousands, you will need to find a direct mailing company.

Your mailing success will be around one percent of the pieces you mail. That means if you mail 100 pieces you will get one person sitting in your seminar room. If your average total mailing per seminar is about 5,000 flyers, you will gather 50 attendees. Your mailing costs will average about .65 cents per mailing. This means that the cost to attract fifty people will be $65 dollars per attendee. This is just the marketing cost, and does not include your hotel room rental or coffee. It does not include any transportation or lodging costs either.

The rental of mailing lists will vary, but they average $.50 per name for business lists depending upon which format you select. Printed peel & stick labels will cost more than if you order a .pdf file. The peel and stick labels you can attach yourself. The .pdf labels would require printing. These are usually trimmed and attached by machine that is much faster than sitting on your office floor with thousands of labels to attach. Been there, done that on many evenings. A professional mailing house can make it easier on you as they design your mail piece, print, address, sort for bulk mail, and deliver it to the post office. Easy to use, but you pay for all this service. Best to handle most of this yourself at first, so you get to know the business and save some money.

All this printing and mailing is simply to let people know that you are offering a seminar. Again, if nobody knows you are offering your seminar, then nobody will show up. Direct mail is not the only way to promote your seminar, but it is the critical first step. It will get the word out first and fast even if most of your flyers go directly into the trashcan as junk mail.

Your task is to reach people who find your topic exciting and who will register for your seminar.

That is why that person who has attended your seminar in the past is gold. They are the ones who will tell their friends that they attended and that it was a great event. Keep your attendee's names and e-mail addresses and continue to build relationships with your past attendees. This will help them see the value of giving you personal referrals. Consider on occasion offering them something that helps cement that relationship. Maybe send them a free book or a well-written informational White Paper. Maybe offer them a discount to attend an upcoming seminar or offer a discount for their friend to attend a seminar. This type of endorsement is worth a lot in future registrations.

We have been talking about using direct mail that is still the standard for many professional seminar firms. It is expensive, but it does pull in attendees. The key is that you have to price your seminar high enough to cover all costs and still bring in profit. Remember you are operating a business and your business either makes money or it goes out of business.

Direct mail still works. It is expensive, particularly if you do not research your SICs. Postage has gone up in recent years and so much of the mailing we send today goes directly in the trashcan. Think about what you do everyday day after your trip to your mailbox. If you are like me, you go through your mail and separate the few pieces you plan to keep. The rest goes directly into your recycle can. That is why it is called junk mail. All mail received is junk unless it fits a specific need at a specific time in your life. When you have a need for training, and a brochure on that topic arrives in your mailbox, you pay attention to it.

Then the Internet arrived. Mailing brochures via the post office can very expensive. As postage and the cost of printing increased, we needed to find another avenue of marketing for seminars. Along came e-mail marketing. With e-mail your marketing costs are much lower. But you still have to conduct research to find your potential audience. This research takes time and time is money.

Remember the difference between junk mail and valuable information. It is the fact that you are known by the receiver as a person with information that is needed by them at that moment. It means that you respect your audience and do not waste their time or money. It is about focusing on their needs, not your own. It is offering quality in all your information products, including the seminar. Your seminar must be worth the price. In fact, it needs to be worth more to your audience than the price you are asking. It must represent a good and attractive deal.

The key to using digital media to promote your seminar has three main features.

First digital media such as e-mail and social media are fast. Within a few minutes of your posting, your audience is reviewing your content. In the old slow snail mail process it could take weeks for the audience to receive your brochure announcing the seminar.

Second is the extremely low cost of communication in a digital sense. Again the old methods cost almost a dollar a piece by the time you rented the list, printed the brochure and paid the postage. You can send your Facebook or Twitter post out literally for free.

Third is the fact that digital marketing allows followers to respond to your message and you have the ability to track your data. This gives you instant feedback on how well you are reaching your audience. With the U.S. Post Office all you knew was the number of returned mail pieces you got back. You were not even sure why they were being returned. In fact, you never knew exactly how many were being delivered to your audience. At least with digital mailing you see those faulty e-mails on your computer screen as rejections or bounces.

These three features of digital seminar marketing, speed of delivery, low cost of reaching your audience and the interactivity of the new media give you an edge that simply did not exist a few years ago.

For years, seminar organizers have been sending out digital flyers announcing their new seminars they were convinced the world needed. It was a sales piece and much of the marketplace considered it spam. Spam is simply unwanted e-mail. It does not matter whether you are sending an announcement through the U.S. post Office or on a digital channel. Junk is junk.

The key to success in seminar marketing is to offer something of value to your audience.

Electronic spamming is the use of electronic messaging systems to send unsolicited messages indiscriminately. You do not want to be considered a spammer. People do not want one more sales person to attack them on the Internet. It is bad enough to have those unwanted phone calls at home during dinner or those envelopes arriving in your daily mailbox. You certainly don't want your e-mail to be full of unwanted spam e-mail.

The key to success in Internet marketing is to start building your own list of names. Your list is made up of two major sources. First it involves asking permission of all your seminar attendees to add them to your prime list. You do this by including a statement on your registration form asking permission to add them to your list. The second list building comes from asking your e-mail newsletter and blog readers to "opt-in" by subscribing to your email list. You need to give people an incentive to give you this permission. The incentive might be a newsletter or updates on your topic. You want to build a list of the people who asked to receive something from you.

Digital marketing requires an active list of potential seminar attendees. This list needs to be grown over time and it is your job to grow that list. You need to start building a responsive list today. Unless you are offering them something of value for their involvement they will not join.

People will not give you permission to add their name to your list unless they see value in doing it.

As you grow your list, you want to add a prospect list. This gives you two lists, a seminar attendee list and a prospect list. You will be working to move people from the prospect list onto the seminar attendee list. Both lists receive the same valuable content, but one is worth more time and attention. The attendee list, which I call my "A list", is where I offer new products and new seminars. I have a much stronger relationship with these people since they have purchased in the past. I will work to sell to this "A" list while I work with the prospect list to build an ongoing relationship.

Amazon.com works this dual list very well. As soon as you purchase a book from Amazon, they will start to suggest other books that you might have an interest in reading. They also suggest that you might want to

126

purchase their Prime Membership that offers free two-day shipping. They are building a relationship with you and they will send you emails on an almost daily basis.

An excellent example of digital marketing can be found at MichaelHyatt.com. Michael offers a variety of marketing tools on his website including a blog and a weekly podcast. He writes his blog on personal development, leadership, productivity, platform and publishing. He also produces a podcast called "This is Your Life" that covers similar topics. His blog appears three times a week and you are asked to subscribe to it via RSS or email. His blog includes a large number of valuable free resources and video clips. Michael also offers his books and seminars in his resource section. Once you are following Michael and gathering all that free content you are likely to purchase his book "Platform" or attend one of his seminars.

Social media such as Facebook, LinkedIn and Twitter are very strong tools for your seminar-marketing venture.

But your email list is still the strongest tool for your seminar marketing. One major problem with building lists on social media sites is that you do not own the list on social media. Facebook, LinkedIn or Twitter owns them. That means that they can change the rules on you at any time. They may be free today, but they could charge a fee tomorrow. They do change the rules every year and they have started to produce advertising opportunities that they offer to sell you. Even though there is value in having friends and connections on social media sites, just be aware that they control you and they could disappear someday. Remember MySpace? Where did it go?

You might consider Facebook advertising. There has been controversy about Facebook ads and its real value and effectiveness. Recently both Ford and Coca-Cola said that they found value in Facebook advertising and that they planned to expand the use of it. One problem with Facebook is that the majority of Facebook users are there to check in on their social lives and not to have you disrupt this viewing. Your ad needs to be quite strong and be able to grab viewer attention. One thing that Facebook says in their advertising guidelines is to "keep it simple" and to explain the benefits of your offer. It might be worth your time to look into this new form of on-line advertising to see if it can add value to your seminar-marketing package.

It is worth enhancing your Internet relationships by offering something for nothing to your list. Michael Hyatt offers a free e-book called "Inside My Tool Box" which gives you "99 resources that will make your business and personal life hum." Michael tells us that these tools are the ones that he uses in his personal and professional life.

It is building your e-mail list that is most critical to you right now.

Michael Hyatt is an e-book for your doing something for him. He is offering you something for doing that "op-in." Jeff Walker in his book *Launch* calls this "op-in" page a "squeeze page." A "squeeze page" is a page that has an "opt-in offer." Jeff says that this offer will help to get someone to join your email list. Your squeeze page and your opt-in offer will be a key to your list building. The thing that makes a "squeeze page" work according to Jeff Walker is that you have a really strong opt-in offer. This is like offering a bribe to get your prospect to join your email list. It must be something of a strong enough value for the person to sign up right now. It can be a video, a White Paper, a free e-book, or anything of value to your prospect. But it needs to have true value and not just be an advertising gimmick.

On your "squeeze page" you might mention a new blog post or podcast that will be highlighting an upcoming seminar or publication. It is smart to offer your audience a discount on your seminar to get them to "opt-in." This helps to build a strong relationship. You will need to start from zero and slowly build followers who want to have a special relationship with you.

I mentioned a blog and a podcast, but have not told you what they are. A blog is a website, usually very personal and an expression of the blogger's passions. A blog is a conversation between you and the reader. A blog is a "web log." That means it is a regularly updated written log posted on the web. It is an online diary with the most recent entries called posts. Each post will have a form for your readers to add their own comments and to leave their opinions or reactions to the post. Your blog lets you get your name out into cyberspace as an expert in the seminar field. Your blog will help to drive people to your online presence. You will need to moderate and respond to comments made to your blog posts.

You might want to look at Guy Kawasaki's blog *"How to Change the World."* Guy calls his blog "a practical blog for impractical people", an interesting thought. Michael Hyatt's blog at *michaelhyatt.com* is focused on "intentional leadership" and his mission is to help leaders leverage their influence. Both of these blogs are intended to lure you into their digital arena and hopefully you will subscribe and eventually purchase materials or attend one of their events.

You can start your blog with free services like Blogger.com, TypePad.com, WordPress.com, or even Facebook.com. If you use text and images on one of these platforms, you have a blog. If you want people to listen to you and you use an audio blog, then you have a podcast. If you use video then you are producing a v-log. But truly, a blog is simply an on-line-based journal with multiple entries.

Blogging will require you to write regularly. You might want to add a new post at least once a week. Some bloggers add a post every day but many bloggers say that is way too often. It will take many readers of your blog a few days to find your new posts and that may lead you to feel that one or two posts a week is best. If your audience enjoys your content, they will return for more. Setting up a blog is the easy part, but writing the blogs on a regular basis is the hard part.

Facebook or twitter can help to drive people to your blog, but it is the blog itself that builds a relationship with your audience. Posts need to be a proper length. The best answer to the proper length is that it all depends. Some bloggers believe that the shorter, the better. Short usually means between 200 to 250 words to a post. Others like a long post of up to or exceeding 2,000 words. It is important to realize that many readers will only read the first few paragraphs of a post. In fact a few studies have shown that most people only read 20% to 28% of a blog post.

A suggested length for each post tends to be between 600 to 1,000 words. If you are writing longer posts, then maybe break them up into several posts. Always start with a catchy headline to excite your reader into starting to read your posts.

Can you sell on your blog? Of course you can monetize your blog. You can sell your own products, be they print books, audiotapes, or e-books. Your readers buy your products, you ship them the same day and their money is deposited into your PayPal account. They can buy from you while you sleep if you are selling digital products.

Working as an affiliate partner is an outstanding way to monetize your blog.

Becoming an affiliate partner with a company like Amazon allows you to sell their books and receive a sales commission. An affiliate partner is a person who promotes another company in return for a commission on sales. Take a look at *launchbook.com/resources* and you will see that Jeff walker is an affiliate marketing partner with a number of companies including ClickBank, WordPress, Skype, PayPal, and Dropbox. It is a good idea to let people know that you have a relationship as an affiliate with these companies and that you receive a commission if they select them through you. This is an honest approach that people will respect.

Can Social Media Help You?

Social media is new to some of you and common practice for others. It is either a tool or toy depending on how you view it. The key in this book is understanding that social media is a strong tool for attracting people to your seminar. It works for both a live and a virtual seminar. Social media is free to use and can be effective for seminar marketing. While it is free to use, it will certainly require time to keep it up to the minute. An outdated social media tool will be extremely ineffective. It will require more than just setting up an account. As soon as your social media becomes out-of-date by even a few weeks, you will lose credibility with your audience.

You have probably all seen Facebook, Twitter, LinkedIn and YouTube. None of these social media sites are over ten years old and they are changing daily. So no matter what I say in this book about social media will be effective for very long. All social media groups have strong membership. Facebook has over one billion members. Twitter has over 500 million members. LinkedIn has over 187 million members and YouTube has over 800 million videos on-line. Those are staggering numbers and the challenge for you is to figure out how to use these sites to promote your seminar.

Just who is viewing social media?

A study by www.onlinemba.com shows the following user stats. These stats will be of interest to seminar promoters. The prime social media tool is Facebook for most seminar attendees. Facebook allows friends to communicate and share with each other online. Facebook is all about connecting people. It's simply a way for people to stay connected with old and new friends as well as for business connections. The important appeal that Facebook will have for those of us in the seminar business is using it as a marketing tool.

The key to marketing with Facebook is to create an effective Facebook Page.

In order to have a Facebook Page that yields measurable results you will need to identify your main purpose or objective. Mari Smith, co-author of *Facebook Marketing: An Hour A Day* tells us "so many small businesses fail to fully benefit from all that Facebook offers quite simply due to a lack of clear goals and a strategy to achieve those goals." Maybe your question should be, why am I on Facebook? What is your goal for marketing your seminar on Facebook? Let's review a few numbers illustrating the demographics of Facebook users.

For Facebook.

* 57% of users of Facebook were female.

* 46% of Facebook users were aged 45 and over.

* Users aged 34 and younger made up 32% of the total.

* 81% of users were college educated.

* 56% had an income of $50,000 or more.

* More than half of the users were doing so on mobile devices such as smart phones and tablets.

A second but very strong social media tool is Twitter. It is a micro-blogging program that allows the publishing of short updates online. These updates are a maximum size of 140 characters or less. Once you publish a Twitter profile for your seminar, you can publish updates whenever you want and about any subject. This might be an announcement of a new seminar or a new seminar date. Twitter is a social networking service that allows you to tell your audience what you are offering. Since it is a short message known as tweets, it works great with mobile technology.

For Twitter

*59% of users were female.

*58% of users were aged 35 or older.

*Users aged 24 and younger made up 19% of the total.

*83% of users were college educated.

*47% had an income of $50,000 or more.

A third major social media tool and one that has a strong business connection is LinkedIn. It is an online professional directory of individuals and businesses. It is different than other social media sites because it's designed specifically for professional networking rather than simply making friends. An interesting fact about LinkedIn is that 44% of its users work in companies with 10,000 or more employees. This is a strong audience for seminars aimed at the corporate market. 39% of its members are managers, directors, chief officers or vice presidents. This group has the ability to send their employees to a variety of seminars. LinkedIn has over 65 million members with the goal of social networking for business purposes. Therefore it is an excellent tool for business-to-business (B2B) marketing.

For LinkedIn

*50/50 split of male/female users

*81% of users were age 35 and over.

*Users aged up to 24 made up 19% of the total.

*87% of users were college educated.

*72% had an income of $50,000 or more.

Social Media and Seminars

Seminar producers use social media for three major reasons. First is to promote their seminars to potential audiences. People who follow on Twitter or share on Facebook or network on LinkedIn will be aware of seminar offerings in their area and can help to announce them to their friends.

Second is the ability to build relationships with connections on their social media accounts. These might be past attendees who found value in your event and are willing to share it with friends online.

Third is the ability to build your seminar brand awareness and recognition through social media placement of your schedule and activities.

The *American Management Association* uses LinkedIn, Twitter and Facebook to share seminar announcements. They have over 10,000 followers on LinkedIn, 234,000 followers on Twitter and over 5,000 Likes on Facebook. They "Tweet" daily hints of successful business practices daily along with suggestions for training opportunities.

National Seminars give weekly E-Tips and they allow anyone to subscribe to these at no charge. Their web page also offers a variety of White Papers as a free download.

SkillPath Seminars uses all of the social media connections, Facebook, Twitter, LinkedIn and YouTube in addition to a blog

Where & When Should You Hold Your Seminar?

This question has multiple meanings. What location is best geographically, what type of facility is the best to hold the event, and what season of the year is best? It depends to some extent whether you are working with a college to offer your event or if you are offering your own public seminar. Let's start by discussing the location first.

If a college or university is sponsoring you, they will pick the location for your seminar.

When you plan your own public seminar it's a whole different ball game. You are responsible for everything. You will miss all the assistance of the college sponsor, but the possibility of earning a higher income may help you relax. The first thing to consider is where you want to hold your seminar. Your first choices are downtown, suburban or an airport location. The critical feature of any seminar location is how easy or difficult it is for your seminar attendees to find you. It is worthwhile considering where the bulk of your attendees are coming from. Are they coming from home or work? You can assume that if your seminar is on the weekend that they will be coming from home and if it is an evening weeknight seminar they will be coming from work. You want to select a site that is convenient for those attending your seminar.

The price that you are charging to attend the seminar and the salary level of your attendees will have an impact on your selection of site.

In order to hold the cost of seminar registration for lower socio-economic attendees you will want to limit yourself to a less expensive facility. If your audience is a higher-income executive group, they will expect a higher-class facility and they can afford it as well. The highest level of corporate executives might require you to hold your seminar at a resort location away from the office.

Each city or resort area has a Convention & Visitors Bureau (CVB) whose task is to help people like us conduct a site search of their area. A site search is a familiarization of their potential seminar locations. The CVB will know intimately each and every property that would be suitable for your seminar. They will ask you what your cost range is and will then be willing to take you on a tour of those facilities. They are well respected by the hotels and it would be a good place to start your site searching. These services are free to the meeting planner and well worth your consideration.

When you select the site for your public seminar you need to consider the population of the area. You will need a significant population to allow you to gain as strong attendance for your seminar. I find that my seminars usually required a city with a minimum population of a million or more residents. In marketing, this gave me the opportunity to gather enough people to produce a profitable seminar.

In selecting the best location it is wise to consider transportation needs. If your audience is coming from work, then holding it near their work locations makes sense. If they are coming from home, then a site in the suburbs might work best. If a large number of your attendees are flying in to the seminar then you might consider an airport location. These airport locations are generally more expensive, but could be much easier for your attendees. Many airport hotels have shuttles and this will ease their parking issues. Parking is a major concern in both airport and downtown locations due to the high parking charges. Check to see what parking costs your attendees will face and see if any discounts are available from the hotels. Ask for a lower rate or complimentary validation.

Partnering With a Hotel

When you contact a hotel property you will be dealing with the sales staff. This sales office is separate from the front desk where you register for a sleeping room. The director of sales or the sales staff knows the property better than anyone else working there. They have the layout down by heart and they have seen all the issues that can arise. Trust their opinion about the best meeting rooms and be ready to ask questions about the services the hotel offers. The sales staff has worked to coordinate many events at their property. For that reason you will find them extremely helpful in arranging the details for your seminar. If you are offering refreshments, you will need to talk to the Food & Beverage Director (F&B). The director of sales might handle this F&B duty in a smaller property.

I do not recommend your supplying food other than coffee, tea and soft drinks for a number of reasons. One is that you will not satisfy everyone no matter how hard you try. The only complaints I ever received on my seminar evaluations were because of the food. Also the food in a hotel always costs more than the restaurant down the street and usually takes longer to serve. It also makes your seminar appear to cost more because you had to add the cost of lunch to the registration. Today, so many people are either dieting or trying to eat healthy that any menu selection is difficult.

I just offer my guests' coffee or tea in the morning and soft drinks at a break. Always announce in your flyer that you are serving coffee, tea and soft drinks. That will alert your attendees that they are responsible to feed themselves breakfast or lunch before attending. Even coffee and soft drinks are expensive when purchased from the hotel. The charge for breakfast in a seminar room generally costs the seminar firm between $20 and $35 per person. This is followed by a 20 percent or higher service charge and the applicable state sales tax. And by the way in many states this service charge is also subject to sales tax. Another issue with meals is that you must give the hotel a final guarantee three days ahead of your seminar. So if someone cancels on you less than three days out, you pay for the meal. You are not allowed to bring any food or drink, including water into the hotel for health reasons. Many hotels charge a labor charge for food service if you have less than 25 guests and this charge could add up to hundreds of dollars.

Be sure to ask how much coffee is per gallon rather than by the cup. Each pot will contain around twenty cups and this is much more reasonable than per cup charges. Many people will grab half cups of coffee and come back for more when it gets cold. If you are charged for each cup you can see how expensive that becomes. Coffee per gallon in a downtown hotel can cost from $60 to $90 per gallon. Be sure to have both regular and decafe available. Bottled water and soft drinks can cost over $5 per bottle so always request tap water on the table with glasses. I think you can understand why I suggest serving only coffee and soft drinks and avoiding all other food.

Another hint with coffee is to tell the hotel to have coffee and tea in the room by 8:30 a.m. and then to refresh it at the first break. Do not tell them to replace the coffee at the first break. You will have coffee left and if you tell them to replace it they will throw away that good coffee. Coffee in those large coffee pots will be fresh all day and it should stay warm as well. Just insure that the coffee is hot when you arrive.

Sometimes the hotel will place the coffee in the room an hour or so before your meeting and it is cold by the time your people arrive. If so, just tell them that you expect hot coffee and ask them to replace it with hot coffee at their expense. I suggest that you request coffee be served in ceramic cups and saucers rather than paper cups. It looks more professional and you want a classy seminar.

As is these days, many of your attendees arrive with a cup of Starbucks. Because of that I usually cut down on the morning coffee since I can always increase the coffee order for the break if needed. I usually do not order coffee for the afternoon break in a full-day seminar since people have hit their limit by then. I find that if they have a need for coffee they will wander down to the local coffee stand and get something like a mocha or tea.

There is no evidence that offering your attendees meals or refreshments will increase registration. What is true that offering food will raise your cost. The hotel makes a high percentage of their income on serving food and the food charges are quite high.

If you do plan on serving any food or beverage, be aware that everything is plus-plus. Plus-plus means that you can expect a service charge and sales tax to be added to your bill. This service charge is not a gratuity or tip. These are not items that you can eliminate if anything goes wrong. Maybe in a restaurant you might lower the tip if the service is sub-standard, but in a hotel meeting room the service charges are mandatory. The sales tax goes to the state and is always added to the bill for any food and beverage service. The plus-plus will generally add at least 30 percent to your bill. Be sure that a clause is in your contract stating that your signature is required on any additions to food & beverage items before you are responsible for payment.

Site Location

Downtown hotels are almost always more expensive than suburban hotels. The reason is that many convention groups book those convenient downtown hotels and the hotels price the meeting space and sleeping rooms and meeting space is generally more expensive than suburban hotels. A suburban hotel will generally be the best bet for less traffic and ease of parking. Most downtown and airport hotels charge for parking and most suburban hotels offer free or low cost parking.

Seminars can be held in hotels, convention centers, community rooms, resort settings, and even aboard cruise ships. Cost becomes a key issue as the rental rates for meeting rooms vary a lot. The location of the facility will also impact the cost, as downtown locations are generally most expensive than suburban locations. For one thing there may be a limited number of hotels with meeting rooms in downtown areas.

Other concerns for your attendees are safety, parking, and transportation. Many inner city areas do not feel safe to your attendees, even if rental rates are lower. Many downtown hotels offer only valet parking and that can be costly. Your attendees may wish to use public transportation and you need to check on the availability of light rail and bus service. Taxi service should be easily available for those who want it.

Start your search on-line and check the major hotel chains such as Hilton, Hyatt, and Marriott. Remember that each of these chains offer lower priced properties that have meeting rooms. For example Hilton has Hilton Garden Inn, Embassy Suites, Hampton Inn & Suites, and Homewood Suites. Hyatt has Hyatt Place and Hyatt House that are smaller and usually less expensive than their more luxury properties. Marriott has Courtyard and Residence Inn locations with smaller meeting rooms at a lower cost.

Depending on the size of your group, these hotels might be better for cost and parking since they are usually found outside the downtown areas. The advantage of using a quality brand hotel like Hilton, Hyatt or Marriott is that it gives your seminar an aura of professionalism. It is a good thought as long as it is not more expensive just because of the name on the flag out front.

Let's look at one hotel in the San Francisco bay area and specifically near the San Francisco Airport. The Hilton Garden Inn is located on the north side of the airport area just three miles from the airport proper. It has 4 meeting rooms with the largest one being 1421 square feet in size and the second largest room being 783 square feet. The largest room can seat 51 in classroom style and the next largest seats 24 classroom style. Both rooms have a 10-foot ceiling. The hotel has free parking and a bus that serves the airport. The hotel was renovated in 2013. They can provide on-site catering and state-of-the-art audio/visual equipment. Wi-Fi is complementary throughout the hotel. I use this as an example of the mid-price properties that are a good choice for smaller seminars. The ceiling height is mentioned because many hotels have a very low ceiling height that might give your attendees a feeling of claustrophobia. Ten feet is the minimum ceiling height I would suggest you to consider using.

This type of information is available on the Internet and should be used prior to calling and visiting the property for an on-site visit. You should do your first search of properties by looking at hotels on the web. Then call the property and request a sales kit that will give you meeting room layouts and prices for both meeting rental and catering services. This information may be available on the hotel website. Make contact with the sales & catering office by phone and ask to check their availability for the dates you have selected.

Ask for any value dates that may be available.

Value dates, also called hot dates, are an economical meeting room price based on space or time availability in the hotel. They know when they are slowest with meetings and they will offer you a discount based on that shortage of customers and un-booked meeting space. Consider shoulder days that are generally Mondays and Thursdays. It may require you to change your seminar date. You might be able to do prior to printing your flyer and it may be worth a substantial cost saving. Remember that it is also smart to negotiate the costs of all hotel costs as none of them are generally in stone. You are a valuable asset to the hotel as their income comes from meetings such as your seminar.

Try to conduct a minimum of 4-6 site visits with those properties that appear to be of high quality and low meeting space rental fees. A site visit is always done in-person and on-site at the hotel. The sales staff member will meet you at the hotel and give you an opportunity to walk the site looking at all aspects of the hotel. The hotel sales kit will have room dimensions and it will help you figure if the room will be large enough for your anticipated group size. I know that the hotel brochure has all the room dimensions but you will be shocked at how your measurements differ from theirs. The hotel will generally host you for lunch that gives you a chance to sample their restaurant offerings, and indirectly to assess their catering service. They will not let you visit a room that currently has a client conducting a meeting but you usually will have an opportunity to sneak a peek in the room. Decide while you are near the meeting room if the location is quiet or if there is noisy air conditioning or personnel.

Ask the costs of both meeting and sleeping rooms by phone prior to your site visit. Then be ready to negotiate against other bids at the end of your site search. Do not pay for a room to be available for a longer period of time than your seminar time. But make sure you would be able to get into the room at least an hour before your seminar starts in order to set up your materials and to arrange any back-of-the-room sales display. You will want to set up your registration tables and place any handout materials in the room. Check that there is enough space outside your meeting room for a registration table if the meeting room space inside is limited. Look at how bright the room lighting is on both the stage area and for attendee note taking. Check to see where the lighting controls are and if you have the ability to control it. At times the lighting and air conditioning controls are in a locked area. Ask if the hotel has an on-sight business center in case you need printing or copying capabilities. As you walk the property look at the condition of the carpet, paint and décor. Walk into the restroom to judge their condition since this will impact your guests. As a final part of the site search, ask for the cost of room rental and any additional charges including food and beverage costs.

After you receive the overall cost is the time to start discussion and negotiations based on your specific needs. This must be done before you sign the final agreement. Ask if a deposit is required and how much is expected. Ask when payment is required and inquire concerning their cancellation policy. Be sure that any costs for the meeting space fits within your overall budget for the seminar. Ask about any discounts available for sleeping rooms for yourself and attendees. Ask if the hotel honors corporate rate discounts for sleeping rooms.

As you walk the various meeting rooms be sure to check on ceiling height and listen to the noise between the walls. Many hotels will tell you that air walls are quiet. Air walls are those walls that are accordion folding walls that allow a room to expand or contract. Being a fabric wall means that you will hear sound coming from the seminar next door. It is good if you can site-search the hotel on a day that has an event in the room next to one you are considering renting. I have had horror stories with all kinds of musical groups or just plain loud motivational speakers located right next door to my room. It is always smart request a solid wall between the seminar rooms for comfort. Nothing is more disturbing than a noisy group next store keeping your people from hearing your presentation.

Check the heating and air conditioning in the meeting room. I have had many rooms that were way too cold or way too hot. Ask the sales coordinator to turn on the heat or air for you to check the quality and ease of adjustment. In many locations, the hotels will eliminate air conditioning once the summer ends, but your meeting room can get stuffy and uncomfortable. Again, you want a ceiling height of at least ten to twelve feet so that the room does not seem claustrophobic. Many hotels convert sleeping rooms into meeting space by combining a number of sleeping rooms into one larger meeting room. The problem is that the ceiling is so low it feels uncomfortable. This is because the average sleeping room usually has only eight-foot ceilings. Be sure that the heating and air-conditioning are not connected to another room for temperature setting.

If you plan to use any audio-visual equipment be sure to check what the hotel has available for rental and what the cost will be for the equipment. Is their projection screens large enough and are they portable or permanently in the room. Is there a charge for the video monitors or projection screens? If you need to work with outside audiovisual rental houses it might get very expensive. I have been in cities where I was not allowed to turn on my power point slides since it was a union hotel. Even though I only used the slides for a small amount of time I ended up paying for an engineer for the entire day. In addition I was required to rent the same equipment that I had with me but was not allowed to use, again by union rules.

If you have an audience larger than fifty you might want to use a microphone. Check to see if the room has poor acoustics making it hard to hear. Ask the hotel what microphones and audio systems they have available and if you have to rent the system or if they are included in the rental price.

Don't be trapped behind a lectern, always use a wireless microphone.

I like a lectern to hold my computer or notes but I want to wander around the room during the seminar. A wired microphone on a stand will limit your movement. I do carry my own wireless microphone that gives more flexibility, but I still need to hook it into their audio system. Be sure that your personal microphone has an XLR connector, as that is the standard connector in professional hotel audio systems. If possible, meet with the hotel technical staff so you can locate the various audio volume controls and get the technician's cell phone number in case of an audio problem. Again ask where you turn on their house audio system and how to adjust the sound levels. Too often I have found these controls located behind a locked door that no one seems to have a key to open.

Make sure that you get everything in writing from the hotel during your site-search. Check this hotel contract for all the details of your meeting. Once you decide on the hotel be sure to get a banquet event order (BEO). This BEO is your contract with the hotel and it will list every part of your seminar event. It will give complete details concerning your rate for the seminar room, your schedule, your food and/or beverage orders, any audiovisual orders, and even the name of your meeting room. This last item is critical since they should not change your selected seminar room without alerting you. If fact they should always ask you permission before attempting to change your seminar room. Remember you took the time to check on that room for quality and you selected it for good reasons. Check the BEO very carefully since you are responsible for anything you may overlook.

Once you have finished a site search for each of your seminar sites, you need to select one property in each seminar location. I put a large map on the wall in the office and using big pins with large colored heads to mark each city that is being considered. The map gives you a quick view of how much travel and time will be involved to complete a seminar season. I mark each city that I was considering offering a seminar in. The map gives you a quick eye view of how much travel and time will be involved to complete a seminar season.

For my own seminar I started with the state of California and began to select the major cities to host one of my seminars. I knew I wanted at least 35-50 people attending at each location. I also knew it would take a minimum mailing of 5,000 flyers in each seminar city to gather those numbers of attendees. The cities chosen were San Diego, Irvine, Santa Monica, Fresno, Sacramento, and San Francisco for the first season. Each these cities were large enough to have the number of attendees and they represented high quality environments. Of course, the first issue was high cost areas for meeting space meant hard work for negotiating came into play for the costs not to exceed budget.

If a college hosts your seminar your seminar season follows the academic calendar. You will be following their fall, spring, and summer class schedules. In that case, offer seminars as early as possible in each college schedule to take advantage of those people signing up early. This early bird approach tends to get those people who want to get back to learning early.

When you start to set your own seminar schedule, your not locked into the college schedule. However following the idea of a fall and spring schedule keeps you in a similar pattern. For many locations winter is more difficult because of weather and holidays. Summer is hard due to everyone's vacation schedules and their children being off from school. People associate learning with school, so September is a great starting time to schedule and go thru mid-December and then start offering seminars again in mid- January and go through May.

Be careful to avoid holiday weekends. So many holidays are celebrated on Fridays or Mondays to give employees a long holiday weekend. The problem is that these are family times and not seminar times. Consider both national and religious holidays when you are planning your seminar schedule. Most people with children will plan vacations around these holidays when their children are out of school. Watch out for the weeks before Christmas, Thanksgiving and Easter for that is again family time.

Avoid as much as you can major sporting events such as the World Series and the Super Bowl. Check on major political events like national elections. If you are holding your seminar in a college town check on the big games and graduation. These events will cause you problems with both attendance and hotel space since those events book lots of hotels for celebrations. The Convention & Visitors Bureau (CVB) are your worker bees, use them for calendar of events for your chosen cities.

If you are holding a seminar aimed at professionals in a certain field such as medical doctors, lawyers, or dentists avoid their major conferences. It just requires a little searching on the web to find all these dates. It is much easier now than it was before the Internet.

After you select the best location is the day of the week that you plan to hold your seminar. Lets start by thinking about which days of the week are best and worst for attracting your audience. Mondays are difficult because everyone is just getting back into the office and they find it harder to get away for a seminar. Fridays are excellent since many people would like to start a long weekend with a seminar. Most folks do not need to return to the office on a Friday afternoon, if the seminar ends a little early. Tuesday, Wednesday and Thursday are equally good seminar days. If you are offering a two-day seminar, Thursday-Friday is a good seminar pattern.

Saturdays are excellent days for personal-development and personal-interest seminars.

Saturdays are better than Sundays, but Sunday afternoons may work well in many locations.

The time you start your seminar depends on the location of the seminar. Traffic patterns and transportation concerns must be considered. In major downtown areas it pays to consider rush hour traffic concerns. You might have a half hour coffee reception to allow those late arrivals to get there and be a little more relaxed before you start the formal seminar. Maybe do introductions or have an icebreaker activity first. If people miss these activities, they are not losing the content they are paying to gather.

Usually a business seminar starts at 8 or 8:30 am since that is when the average person gets into the office. A personal-development seminar on the weekend starts at 9 am to allow your attendee to relax on that morning a little more.

I usually start my registration at 8:30 am and the seminar starts promptly at 9:00 am. The three-hour seminar takes a break in the middle for ten to fifteen minutes for going to the restroom and enjoying coffee and social time. The full day seminar starts at the same time but usually breaks early for lunch at 11:30 am. This allows people to get to local restaurants before the majority of outside diners get there. Breaking early also helps to insure that your guests will return for the afternoon session on time that starts at 12:30 p.m.

Be sure to let your people know where local and affordable restaurants are and if they are in close walking distance from the seminar. Your hotel contact can provide this information and a map. Many times the hotel you are holding the seminar in will have a restaurant on property. You might check to see if that hotel restaurant will offer your attendees a discount on their lunch. It is a good idea on a full-day seminar to try to complete the seminar no later than 4 pm to give your people an opportunity to get on the road before major traffic time. It will also help if a few of your attendees need to catch a flight home.

Personal-development seminars are best either on Saturday or in the evenings. If you hold your seminar in the evening, you should plan to hold it on a Tuesday, Wednesday, or Thursday night. Any of the three are equal for attendance. It is best to start registration at 6:30 pm with the seminar starting at 7 pm. This will let people have a quick dinner before heading to the seminar. For an evening seminar, no coffee or refreshments are required; water pitchers and glasses on each table are sufficient. An extra thought is for you to join the hotel brand loyalty program. As a member you will earn free hotel nights and exclusive benefits such as faster check-ins and room upgrades.

Delivering Your Seminar

You have spent months preparing for this day! You sat at your computer writing the seminar copy, followed by months planning the marketing, and you ran around town finding the perfect location to house your seminar. Now it's time to go on stage and wow that audience. Hopefully you have been receiving registrations for the past few months. You have answered everyone's questions about the seminar online and on the phone. You have used PayPal or Square to accept credit card payments in advance. You have received many registrations and you have gathered them all in a folder and have built a list of registrants for each seminar offering. This is the list you will have available at the registration table to check people off as they arrive.

You hired or begged someone to sit at the registration table and smile and say good morning to each person as they arrive. They will give each guest your agenda, direct them to the coffee and indicate where the restrooms are located. You have set up a

display table near the coffee that displays all the
items that your attendees will purchase to take home
with them. You also have placed a display of one of
each item on the stage so that your people can see
them throughout the presentation.

You gave each attendee an evaluation form as they
signed-in. This simple one page form will give you an
opportunity to see how your guests feel that each
section of your seminar is doing. It is a critique that
you will use to improve your seminar. I like to read
these on the flight home and hopefully most of them
are positive in nature. You will receive a few critical
ones that you will learn from and use to adjust your
next event. The added value of these evaluations is
having your attendees give comments that can be
used in your future marketing.

If you plan to use these testimonials to promote
upcoming seminars, be sure to ask permission from
the evaluators. Put a checkbox on the evaluation
form that asks if you can use their comments in
future marketing. Most people will give you

permission but if they say no, follow their refusal by not using their comments. When you add their comment to your marketing tool, be sure to use their name and company or just use their first name and last initial. This testimonial is worth many dollars of value because people read them. It is like using *Travel Advisor* or *Open Table* and checking what people say about a hotel or a restaurant before you make your reservation.

It is helpful to give each person a list of attendees that have signed up for the seminar. It is a good idea to let people know that you are planning to give this out and give them the option of not having their names or companies appear on the list. You should alphabetize the names on the attendance list. Each person should be given a self-adhesive pre-printed name badge. This name badge label should be at least 2 x 3 inches in size with their names printed by computer. The names should be large enough to be read at a distance using at least 18 point type. Use an easy to read typeface such as Cambria or Century Schoolbook. Clip on name badges are better protection for most fabrics, but are slightly more expensive and time consuming to produce.

Leave enough time for people arriving to network with other attendees.

You might state that the doors open for networking and refreshments at 8:30 a.m. and the seminar starts at 9:00 a.m. This will allow people to mingle and will allow for late arrivals. You should be at the door to welcome your guests as they arrive and to introduce yourself as the presenter. If you plan to have all participants introducing themselves at the beginning of the seminar, let them know that as they arrive. It will help them prepare a short elevator speech and maybe eliminate the nervousness that everyone has when speaking in public.

Before your people arrive, check the room temperature. Just remember that as more people arrive, the room always seems to get warmer and you may need to re-adjust it. In hotels, the temperature

174

control settings are usually in a locked box and will need to be adjusted by hotel staff. Find out where the temperature control is located and see if it is locked. If the temperature is not locked, you might ask the hotel to lock it because quite often one of your attendees might become the room temperature monitor and that is not a good idea. This monitor usually makes the room too warm or cool for the majority of your guests.

Most hotels have become non-smoking, but it is a good idea to mention that your seminar is non-smoking. Second-hand smoke is both unhealthy and annoying to the majority of your guests. If the hotel has ashtrays in the meeting room, simply remove them. Mention at the beginning of the seminar that if any guests wish to smoke they would have to do it off the hotel property.

Check the lighting in the room when you arrive and have the hotel staff adjust it if it is not properly set. Check both the lighting on stage as well as the lighting for your guests to take notes. You do not want the lighting on the audience to be too bright as many people will be using their tablets or computers for note taking and lighting that is too bright will make that difficult.

Many presenters will stay at the hotel the night before the seminar to insure a good rest and to avoid the possibility of being late for their own seminar. Check to see if the hotel can offer a professional rate or a complementary sleeping room. This is critical if you are flying in for your seminar, as many flights are delayed or cancelled.

Regardless of whether you are staying the night before or traveling in on that day, plan to arrive early.

You need to insure that all the hotel signage is correct for your seminar. Many times I have found that the hotel had forgotten to post the seminar on their event wallboard. You also want to check on any audio or visual equipment that you are planning to use. Locate the rest rooms and emergency exits so that you will be able to direct your guests to them. You might wish to place any handout materials on the tables and it is helpful to do that before anyone arrives.

Meet with the hotel support staff just before your seminar to insure your agenda and any food and beverage service you have contracted for are correct. Let the catering staff know that only you can order anything and not your guests. Your guests might wish to order something from hotel catering and that is their personal responsibility to pay for and it should not be added to your bill.

Be sure to tell your guests to turn off their smart phones, and remind them that they should step out into the lobby to take any calls. That is a common courtesy and your guests will appreciate that request. If the hotel has music playing in your meeting room be sure that it is soft easy-listening classical music. That will create a welcoming environment for your guests. Find out how to silence the music when the seminar is ready to begin. Find out if you have control of it or if you need to alert the hotel staff to do it.

You should always dress slightly better than your audience. If your guests will be arriving in business causal attire, then you should be in a suit or dress. It is a good idea to suggest attendee dress in your seminar brochure. This will relax your guests on how to dress for your event.

When you state the starting time for your seminar, then start at exactly that time.

Don't cause guests who arrived on time to wait for late arrivals. If you plan an icebreaker activity then start it on time and tell people exactly when you will call them all back together again.

You are the Star!

You are the rock star for the day and you need to start with lots of energy. Show your enthusiasm and begin by telling a fun story or an interesting thought for the day. Don't start with a joke. Jokes might cause someone in the audience to be upset and many people do not get the point of the joke anyway. Stories from your personal history are much better and will give your audience a warm feeling.

As the presenter you must have a compelling message and a forceful delivery. Speaking to any size group is going to give you a nervous feeling. That is normal. The key to becoming a better presenter is to simply practice your presentations numerous times. The more you practice, the better you present.

You should script your entire presentation. In building your script follow the philosophy of getting it down and then getting it right. At this point do not worry about proper spelling or grammar. It may be messy but it is the right place to start, just getting it down. You will go back later and make it pretty. The idea of "less is more" will help you to edit your material. You might have too much material at first and you will need to edit it down to a three-hour version.

Start your seminar by letting your attendees know the seminar agenda. This will prepare them for what is coming. Think of your presentation as a conversation that you are having with your audience. Conversations have value. Your content is there to help them. Organize your material in a series of steps that are easy to present and easy for your audience to follow. Organize your material as steps or keys. Your seminar might be organized as seven steps or seven keys. Make each step complete with a beginning, middle and end.

When you start your presentation, tell yourself to slow down.

Slow down your presentation speed because many people talk too fast because they are nervous. Talking too fast is difficult on your audience. Remember that they are trying to understand you and at the same time take notes. Please be nice to them and talk slower.

The key to speaking well is to remember to pause at least once in each sentence. Pause longer than it feels comfortable and it will probably be the right length of pause. A pause does a couple of important things for you and the audience. First it lets them think about what you just said. It gives them a "thinking break." Second it gives you a chance to take a breath. So do not only slow down you're speaking, but also add pauses in each sentence.

Use notes even if you know your material well. The problem with memorizing lines is that when someone in the audience asks you a question and you try to get back into your script, you may have no idea where you were. Notes are not there for you to read, they are to keep your content flow in the right direction. Your notes might be only keywords. These keywords are to help you remember the proper sequence. You might use your computer on the lectern with your notes on it. The audience cannot see the computer, but you can gaze at it to see your notes. You can use an electronic clicker to advance the slides and it is so small that the audience does not notice you clicking it to advance your note pages. I use a Kensington wireless presenter that costs less than sixty dollars. You need it to be either a PC or Mac version.

I suggest that you allow questions from your audience whenever they arise. It is unfair to expect your guests to hold their questions until the end of your talk. It is helpful to have someone available with a microphone to approach the guest with a question. Otherwise the audience will not be able to hear the question. If you do not have that person to approach your guest with a microphone, you should always repeat the question. This will allow your audience to hear the question and to insure that you understand the question. Repeating the question will give you a few minutes to think of the answer. It is never wrong to say that you don't have an answer, but you will find the answer and get back to the person. If you promise that, be sure that you get their e-mail address.

Your presentation should resemble a conversation with the audience. Conversation is always relaxed. In a conversation you normally ask a question when you see a person look confused. Get in the habit of asking for questions throughout your presentation, not waiting until the end of the seminar.

Always schedule breaks every hour or so. People have rest room, coffee and cell phone needs. Nothing is more bothersome to your guests than not breaking often enough. Usually it is the presenter's fault by not scheduling enough breaks. It is a good idea to let your audience know when you plan for breaks. Let your people know how long the breaks are. Keep your word and start back when you say you the break is over. The problem with not starting back on time after breaks is that it wastes time. And you will have to shorten your program because you run out of seminar time.

Keep your smart phone or a timer on the lecturn to allow you to schedule breaks and your ending. You must end on time because your guests have a schedule to keep. Ending a few minutes early is appreciated by many and gives everyone a chance to ask questions and to purchase your back-of-the-room materials.

Plan an exciting ending to the seminar and then thank everyone for attending.

Recognize any sponsors and staff. Ask for any last minute questions before you do your close. This will allow everyone to hear your well-planned close after you bring their attention back following their questions. Let them know that you will be in the back of the room to sign books and answer questions for as long as they wish to stay. These are your best friends and you should not rush off.

You might give each attendee a seminar workbook with space to take notes. This workbook should include a list of the common words for your topic and also a series of references. These references will include publications available.at Amazon.com. Use Amazon.com because you should be an affiliate member of Amazon so that when your participants order any publications you get a commission.

Ask your hotel if they can supply pens at no charge to your participants. Many people arrive without writing instruments or even note paper. Hotels are usually interested in this because the pens advertise the hotel.

Check to see if the hotel offers Wi-Fi for you to use during your seminar. Many hotels have free Wi-Fi, but not in the meeting rooms. In the meeting rooms it may be an added cost.

Added Profits: Back-of-the-Room Sales

Would you like to double your profit each time you offer a seminar? Are you curious? All you need to do is offer back-of-the-room items to your attendees.

The key to successful and profitable back-of-the-room sales is to offer items that are wanted and hard-to-get.

Do not sell books that the audience can get for a discount at every Sam's Club. That will anger the folks as soon as they see them on your table. You need to offer items that that they have never seen before.

Let's start with a seminar workbook. This is a 3-ring binder full of notes, references, and even a printed copy of your PowerPoint slides. These are slides that they have never seen since they are your instructor notes. It will contain dividers for each section of your seminar and it will become a desktop reference when they get home. I even add a flip drive to it with copies of all my handouts. These handouts might include magazine reprints and a short essay that you authored for them. The reference section would include a listing of all the critical publications on the topic of the seminar. This section might include the associations and local Meetups in this field. It will include everything your attendee could use to find the critical people to contact. It includes numerous checklists and sample forms.

In your college sponsored seminar this workbook is required reading material and everyone who takes your seminar buys it. It must be used during and after the seminar to qualify as required material. You will charge a fair price for this item. I charge twenty dollars for my seminar workbooks. The cost of production is around six dollars and therefore I add about fourteen dollars per student to my seminar income. Most colleges will add your materials to their catalog as "material fees" and they expect your participants to pay you on the day of the seminar for the workbook. A few colleges will add that fee to the class registration fee.

Be aware that in many states you must charge sales tax on anything you sell at your seminar and then you must file your tax return with your state franchise tax board at the proper time. A few states allow you avoid charging sales tax if the materials are consumable, meaning they are used in class. Check with your college or state franchise tax board about the sales tax requirements. If the state requires you to collect sales tax on your materials, you will also have to apply for a state sales tax permit to collect and pay the sales tax. Be careful not to get yourself in trouble over a little tax that you owe the state. This is state sales tax and not income tax which you will need to report and pay based on your seminar income.

Back of the room materials include more than just your seminar workbook. It could include a variety of items that you feel would help your participants after the seminar. This might include audio CDs, DVDs, blog subscriptions, and other books that you or someone else authored. Many publishers will allow you a reseller's discount since you are a retailer selling materials for your seminar. But never sell the materials for more than the retail price.

Audio CDs are a perfect sales item that you can produce yourself. Many people would like to avoid note taking, and still have your seminar to listen to again and again. You can record a seminar live or simply record it at your desk and bring copies to the seminar to sell. These CDs sell for between 10 and 30 dollars and are extra income to you. DVDs are certainly more effort to produce, but the new smart phone digital cameras and webcams allow you to produce them yourself right at your desk. We will talk soon about actually doing a virtual seminar with a webcam and never leaving your office.

Let's discuss how to successfully sell back-of-the-room materials. You should display your materials at a site near your registration table. This allows your attendees to see the materials as they arrive and register for your seminar. Avoid any hard sell! The best way to sell is to mention the value of a product during your presentation. In fact, hold the item up during the seminar and mention that it will be useful to them following the seminar. Mention that you use the item all the time, and by the way, you brought a few along and they are at the back of the room. Get the idea? We are selling them by promoting the value of the item and then letting them know that we can supply them today. It's a good idea to read a short passage from your book during the seminar as that allows you to mention the book one more time. Offer to sign the books during the breaks and after the seminar. People enjoy having the author put a personal note in the book.

If you hold a game during your seminar you might offer the winner a book as a give-away. Always select someone as a winner who is seated near the back of the room. You might ask a question and the first hand near the back of the room wins a copy of your book. By passing the book all the way to the back of the room it automatically passes through many hands. It allows you to give away your book and at the same time allow many people to see it.

It is smart to only place a few of your products on the back table. Scarcity sells. People tend to be more interested in things that are in short supply. They will rush to purchase your items at the first break, if not before your seminar starts. Bring your products in amble supply, but keep the extra products hidden until they are needed. But be sure to bring enough product so as to not disappoint people. It is a good idea to also have your products on display on a table in the front of the room so that people are seeing them all day long. You want to bring them up just before the first break. But be careful not to over sell them, just let your audience know that they are useful tools for them to enjoy after the seminar.

How many people will buy products at a seminar? It is hard to estimate what number of anything will sell. The best estimate is that everyone in the room will buy one item. That does not mean each individual will actually purchase a book, but that you will sell 50 books if you enroll 50 people. Many people buy multiple copies or sets of products. So the general rule is that you should figure on selling 50 books, if you have 50 attendees. Bring enough product with you, but not too much. If you are traveling a distance you may need to ship the products in advance and this is a cost factor for the seminar.

It is a good idea to offer your books in bundles.

You could package six different books in a bundle at a discount. Where the books might sell for $20 each, you might offer all six for $97. This is a good discount, and it does entice a number of people to purchase all six books, especially if you take credit cards or are willing to bill their company . In the old days, even five years ago it was very expensive to offer credit card sales. Your bank had to offer you that service and then they charged a monthly fee, plus a per-sale charge. It almost was not worth it. Today all of us can accept credit cards via Square or PayPal.

Square accepts credit cards using your smart phone or IPad. All you do is sign up at www.squareup.com and request a free reader. Then download the Square Register app that works with Square Reader. This Square Reader turns your smartphone or iPad into a mobile point of sale. After registering your Square account, you simply plug in your Square Reader, sign in to Square Register and start swiping your attendee's credit card. There are no monthly fees or commitments. Square accepts all major credit cards.

Another way to accept those credit cards and other types of payments is with PayPal. Many of your attendees will have PayPal accounts and it will let them purchase with their credit cards or bank accounts. You can add PayPal to your checkout system. It is a low fee per transaction and is used by over 150 million users. You can accept all major credit cards and use the PayPal reader on your smart phone. Simply go to paypal.com to sign up as a PayPal merchant and get the card reader and smart phone app.

Like Square and PayPal, Amazon has its own plastic credit card reader called Amazon Local Reader. Amazon's new credit card reader plugs into the headphone jack of mobile phones and tablets, just like those made by Square, PayPal, and a range of other companies. The reader works in tandem with a mobile app that, along with handling the basic transaction, gives you access to data on sales trends, peak sales times, and more.

Sell your products before, during, and after your seminar. Many people come to your seminar looking for tools to help them after the seminar. Others will be convinced by you during the seminar that the products will help them after they return home. Many people want to take the presenter home and taking their products home meets that demand. Make sure that you make it easy for them to purchase your products. Credit cards, accepting checks and even being willing to bill them after the fact will increase your sales. Remember that you will likely double your days income with simple back-of-the-room products.

The Virtual Seminar

How can you present a seminar in virtual space? Just what does that mean? You hear about distance learning, webinars, and virtual presentations. Can you really give a seminar from your office to a group of people who are not present? The answer is yes and that seminar can be very effective. Web seminars are meetings conducted over the internet between any size of audience. Using high-speed internet connections allows your audience to attend your seminar anywhere across the globe. A virtual meeting pays no attention to geographical boundaries or even time zones. This technology of web meetings became popular after the terrorist attacks of 2001 which put limits to conferences and airline travel. A web meeting allows your attendee to relax at home or in their office or even attend the meeting while on the road.

It is important to realize that all of the same rules for giving an effective in-person seminar apply to a virtual one. But let's be honest, many virtual presentations are just plain boring. They are simply talking PowerPoints with too many words and too much talking. Web meetings also require that the attendee have suitable hardware, software, and internet connectivity. While this was a problem back in 2001, almost everyone today has a smart phone, tablet or desktop computer with an internet connection. It will take some of your potential attendees time to adjust to virtual seminars because they are expecting to attend a live seminar.

The key to a strong virtual seminar is to keep it as short as possible, maybe 60 minutes max.

If you need it longer, produce a series of presentations with breaks between segments. In a live seminar it is easier to hold your audience's attention. Make the virtual presentation as visual as you can by including video clips and pictures. Maintain a brisk pace using your best narration voice or even use multiple presenters to gather audience attention.

Many people call a virtual presentation a webinar. You can also call it a web conference, online seminar, e-seminar, or a web seminar. A virtual seminar is simply communication between the presenter and an audience over the internet. It can use audio, PowerPoint, or even video to communicate your message. They are a form of seminar, but it appears very different to your audience. Going to a seminar, particularly if it requires an out of town trip can be quite exciting. A day or more out of the office and an opportunity to meet other professionals, maybe over a glass of wine. Many people might find the virtual seminar a boring experience. This may be because they have experienced just that, a boring virtual seminar. Virtual seminars do not have to be boring. A number of national seminar companies are offering exciting virtual events. Here are a few of these seminar providers.

National Seminars offers webinars which they stress as

effective training, the quick and easy way. They offer one-hour trainings which you can use with your entire staff for one price. For example, they offer *Presentation Tips: Tips for Creating Visually Engaging Slides*, a one hour webinar for $179. If you cannot attend the scheduled webinar, you may purchase a CD-ROM of the seminar. If you enroll in the webinar, you will have the opportunity to submit questions via e-mail. Time permitting, they will address questions from webinar participants.

Fred Pryor Seminars offers a variety of one-hour webinars. One webinar is *"Bad E-mail Habits: What Message Are You Sending?"* It tells us that it can help us to eliminate embarrassing mistakes that damage your organization's credibility. This webinar includes the CD-ROM and costs $248. Another webinar offered by Fred Pryor seminars is *"What NOT to Say to Your Customers."* They tell us that this seminar is designed for people who face customers regularly including retail salespeople, sales professionals, servers and any other job with a focus on customer service. The one hour webinar will cost their clients $199.

The American Management Association offers free online webcasts simply by registering for them. This is a method for gathering e-mail addresses from people who show an interest in the topics. This tool will then be used to promote paid webinars and live seminars. Their live seminars are generally two or more days held in a variety of locations and may cost the attendee over $2000 dollars depending whether you are a member of the association or not.

The challenge in a webinar is to keep it from becoming a boring event

The concept of a boring presentation can occur in a live seminar as well, but it seems to be much more likely to occur during a virtual presentation. Many times it is boring only because it consists of too much type on the screen. Too many words on the screen at one time, and presenters who read every word out loud to their audience. Your virtual seminar attendees are generally sitting in their office with all that possible disruption from e-mails and other people wanting their attention. These office distractions might make it harder for the virtual seminar attendee to hold their attention on the webinar.

It is helpful to remember that visuals in presentations started years ago with photographic slide presentations. The presenter had a photographer or audio-visual expert produce a set of slides to illustrate a seminar. Each slide cost a few dollars to produce because the photographer may have shot a roll of film or more to produce the perfect slide. The cost may have been up in the hundreds of dollars per slide. You were limited in the number of visuals you could show because of the cost. Then along came Microsoft and they produced PowerPoint as part of their Office suite.

It was PowerPoint that became so easy to use and it was inexpensive to produce thousands of slides. We started having what are referred to as "slide decks" which allowed all presenters to overload their presentations with too much text and visuals. In fact, we started to have rules for PowerPoint slide decks. One rule told us no more than six words per line and no more than six lines of text on each PowerPoint slide. Do you realize that meant that a slide could have 36 words on the screen at one time and still meet that rule. And that was the minimum number of words and you know that many slides exceed that number. Wonder why audience members go to sleep and stop listening to the presenter?

Virtual seminars involve both the presenters voice and a group of visuals. The verbal component or the voice of the presenter is no different on a virtual presentation than during a live one. The presenter must command attention during either format. A dull speaker is a dull speaker in either mode. It is easier for the audience to stay energetic during a live presentation since they have direct contact with you. If you are simply in a studio or sitting at your desk it is much more difficult to keep them alert for an hour's presentation.

One advantage to a virtual seminar is that it can be recorded and anyone who missed it the first time could view it later.

Your attendees can watch the seminar a second time when they return to the office or even at their home. Since you are charging for the seminar, you can give your audience a password to access and view the seminar multiple times.

WebEx, a virtual conference firm estimates that more than 12 million web meetings and training sessions take place everyday. Just how many of these web meetings have been effective is a good guess. Well just how many live meetings have been effective? And what does being effective mean? Can a meeting be boring and still be effective? I certainly hope not, but the chance of a virtual meeting being boring is no higher than a live meeting being boring. Web seminars are not better or worse than a live seminar, they are just a different medium.

So what are the advantages of a web seminar?

1. Better use of everyone's time as travel is eliminated. Even though many individuals might enjoy travel and the opportunity to be out of the office, it still costs attendee time. As the presenter you are able to stay in your office and present the seminar. You also have the ability to schedule each seminar multiple times which is much more flexible for your attendee's schedules. How many times have you wanted to attend a seminar, but it was scheduled at the same time as another important activity.

2. There is no limit to the number of participants you can

speak to virtually. You are not limited by the size of the meeting room and you do not have to turn down attendees because the meeting room has exceeded the local fire code.

3. You can record the presentation and on a regular basis you can present it again. It is easy to store your virtual seminar. You can also allow your attendees to review the seminar and catch anything they may have missed. How many times in a live seminar does your attendee get an important phone call or need a rest room break and miss a critical piece of your information?

4. It is easier to present critical video without the expense of high quality video projection and Wi-Fi availability. The rental of this capability is quite expensive and is required at each live presentation. How often have you experienced problems with the set-up of audio-visual technology at the seminar site. You spend time waiting for the local techie to get things working while you do a soft shoe dance for the audience.

5. You save the cost of the facility to hold the seminar, as well as the cost of your travel. You will normally have travel, lodging, and meal costs as you travel from seminar location to seminar location. A large cost is the rental of the meeting room and any food & beverages you offer.

Let's discuss a few challenges in holding a virtual seminar.

1. If we believe that over 85 percent of communication is nonverbal, then it is an issue when you cannot see the presenter live. You might use video on-site to allow your audience to watch you perform.

2. It may seem more difficult with virtual media to gather rapport with your audience. As an in-person presenter you will be moving around the room and being able to answer questions rapidly. This tends to produce a more favorable relationship. By using a telephone or webcam in each location your

attendee could ask questions which gives the virtual seminar a live feeling. But maybe a few audience members might just as soon remain invisible to you and a virtual seminar would be welcoming to them.

3. Some of your audience will feel they lack the technical ability to operate a virtual seminar. They might be afraid of the technology or even fearful that they might do something harmful to their technology. Even the presenter might worry that the technology could go down during a virtual event, but you need to be aware that this can happen in both live and virtual situations. Many times during a live seminar, the video or audio system will fail leading to a delay while the local tech help is found.

4. Even though you can get distracted during a live seminar, it is probably more likely to occur if you are in your office. The normal work environment

will be going on while you attend a virtual seminar. You might feel the need to respond to e-mails or texts while tuned into the virtual seminar. True, with smart phones this can occur while sitting in a live seminar.

5. You may find that it is difficult to have a high level of participation during a virtual seminar. In the live seminar you can see that hand go up to ask a question. You will not have direct eye contact with your audience.

It is important to remember that the purpose of a virtual seminar is not just to present information.

If that is your goal you would be better to produce a "White Paper" and e-mail it to your audience. You are looking for a two-way conversation with your audience. In a virtual seminar you have the ability to take questions with internet voice or via chat. You need to be aware that a virtual seminar is new to many members of your audience. You may want to instruct your audience how to send questions to you. This training at the beginning of the virtual seminar will increase the amount of interaction you receive.

Most of us have presented to live audiences, maybe not in a seminar setting, but certainly in a one-on-one meeting. It may be the use of new virtual technology which will give you that nervous feeling. All of us at times grow nervous making a presentation, live or virtual. But the virtual technology adds a new element to our concern. We worry that the software might crash, or that the attendee's computer might freeze or the audio might go mute. Much of this nervousness comes from having to work with a new form of technology.

Virtual seminars require a computer, the internet, and software. There is a large variety of web presentation software out there for you to consider. Even after you select the software, it will continue to upgrade itself multiple times, giving you another learning curve to adjust to. This book will not suggest a specific software or teach you to use it. But we will discuss what is required in hardware and software to have a successful virtual seminar. All software companies offer training in the particular features of that product.

There are two basic types of platforms for virtual seminar applications. Browser-based and server-based applications. You can do it yourself or hire a webinar service. The cost can vary from inexpensive to quite costly.

Browser-based applications run from your desktop, therefore what's on your screen is what your audience sees. A popular version of a browser-based program is *GoToMeeting*. It can handle up to 100 attendees and deliver video conferencing. It can be used by your attendees on their desktop or with IOS and Android apps on their smart phone or tablet. You can use a webcam to see everyone face-to-face. It is possible to record your seminar, both the video and audio. For larger audiences you might consider *GoToWebinar* which allows up to 1000 attendees. Both of these systems allow your attendees to easily join the webinar in seconds. All your audience needs to do to join the seminar is to click a link in the confirmation e-mail that you sent them.

Server-based applications require you to upload your presentation to a central server and it goes to your participants from there. This is practical for a large-scale event with up to 3,000 participants. Because it is sent by the platform provider, you are less likely to have technology failures. This system allows up to 125 callers to respond with questions or comments during the seminar. You can allow your participants to view the attendee list and also give them an evaluation form at the conclusion of the seminar. Examples of server-based software is *WebEx* and *Adobe Connect*. One advantage of the server-based platform is that they are very stable since you are not depending on your own computer technology.

The key is to understand which platform you will use and what features are available on that platform.

Then spend the time to practice with your specific platform and get comfortable with it. I feel that anything you can do in a face-to-face seminar can be done in a virtual format.

Self-service or Full-service

If you are planning a web-seminar where you are using your own webcam, you can do it yourself without much concern. But if you are planning a virtual seminar where you have large numbers attending and you plan to record it, you might consider the more involved full-service model.

The suppliers that were mentioned earlier are today's key players in software for a virtual seminar. They are *Adobe Acrobat Connect Pro*, *WebEx*, and *Go To Webinar*. By the time you read this book there will be numerous changes to these programs and no doubt many new offerings. But the concept will be the same for all virtual seminars. All three listed above are web conferencing platforms for holding web meetings, e-learning and webinars. They will allow you to deliver compelling seminars and will drive registration with password event entry.

One critical factor is to be sure to select webinar software that can handle the size of audience you plan to attract. Are you looking for 50 or 500 participants? For example *GoToMeeting* allows up to 100 participants, while their sister software *GoToWebinar* allows 1,000 people to participate.

If you plan to do the set-up yourself, you will want to invest in software that allows easy set up without calling in the IT department. You should select a program that works with both PCs and Mac. It is important to have Chat so that you can exchange instant messages and e-mails with your participants. It is also handy to be able to send group messages and e-mails during the presentation.

It may be important that you archive the seminar by recording and posting it to your website. This will allow people to enroll who cannot attend at your scheduled time, but can attend at a later date. You are allowing people to attend your seminar without leaving their work place or they could take it at home.

A major advantage for the virtual seminar is that you are able to offer your seminar literally world-wide. There is no limit, short of language, to global attendance. This medium also allows the addition of video and audio recording without the high cost of projection video equipment onsite. It allows you to add PowerPoint and streaming video into your seminar.

Virtual seminar registration is simply a matter of going online, signing up with a credit card and then waiting for the seminar to start. Your attendees might have to supply their own coffee, but they could even enjoy your seminar sitting at their local Starbucks. Since the seminar registration gives each participant their own password there is strong security that insures that only those who have registered and paid will be attending. The value of this virtual seminar is that you can offer the seminar to any number of attendees since your cost has been reduced by eliminating the meeting room rental. You deliver the seminar either live from your office or it was recorded at an earlier date.

The fear that many people have about virtual seminars is that the technology will be difficult to learn or that it may fail during your event. All of the webinar software firms mentioned in this book have excellent and low-cost training to get you up and running.

Remember that you will feel at times that you are all alone on the stage with a webinar. It will seem difficult to gauge your audience reactions to your presentation. Start your learning curve by attending as many webinars and on-line seminars as you can before you begin offering yours. There are many virtual online seminars that you can join. See what works in these events and take many notes about what you think works and what doesn't work. Look at the various software and platforms they are using and what tools and functions they are applying.

The visual component of a virtual seminar is extremely important but so is the audio component. The audio usually involves using either using telephone or a Voice Over Internet Protocol (VoIP). All your attendees have a landline or a cell phone that they might use for seminar communication, but a headset is more effective. The attendees should be told to mute their phones to avoid any background sound. The Voice Over Internet Protocol (VoIP) requires a microphone and a headset. You will need to tell your attendees to turn off their computer speaker or it could cause feedback. You will need to insure that all your attendees have a Wi-Fi broadband connection.

By now you may be asking what it will take to convert your live presentation into a successful virtual seminar. It is important to realize that the key difference is that you are not in the room with your audience. You are not face-to-face with them. One strong suggestion is to limit your seminar to 45 minute segments with at least a 10 minute break between segments. In a live seminar you can go for over an hour or even an hour and a half. In a live seminar this break gives people an opportunity to network, get coffee, and use the restroom. The virtual seminar audience still needs time to refresh their coffee and visit the restroom, but no real networking is available. This will allow a much shorter break between segments.

It's Your Time to Start

Thank you for reading this book. Even though I have authored a number of books, my true passion is in developing and offering seminars. Some days I am not sure whether it is more fun developing the seminar or being on the stage delivering it. This book is written to give you the knowledge and confidence to build your first seminar, live or virtual. It will take months of work to produce that successful seminar. It does take a lot of work.

Planning a seminar is like writing a book. It is a lonely act. Your friends might listen to you describe your planned seminar, but when it comes right down to it, you will make all the decisions by yourself. You will question many of your decisions multiple times and not really know the correct answer until you test the seminar with a live or virtual audience. I have attempted to show you the step by step process of designing and marketing a seminar. But it will be your seminar and you need to make all the decisions. Expect to make mistakes and to learn as you design the seminar. Expect it to be more work than you anticipate. Expect many frustrations and late nights. But get ready to stand up and cheer when that first seminar is over, and your attendees clap and thank you as they leave your seminar room. It will be exciting to have all those people waiting to discuss your topic with you following your seminar. They will become your personal fan club.

It is time for you to start planning that first seminar. You have attended seminars, both live and virtual. As you sat in those seminars, you were either filled with excitement or you were bored silly. You wondered exactly what made the difference. Was it the presenter? Was it the topic, or was it the how the seminar was organized? Did the location make a difference? Was the seminar too long or too short? Was the seminar too expensive or was it too cheap? Did the presenter make it interesting? These are the questions that will be running through your mind as you start to plan your own first seminar.

You will make mistakes. I admit that I am still learning this seminar business. It is a different business. I have had seminars that were cancelled because of low attendance, and seminars that had more people show up than the room could handle. I had to stop seminars because of hotel fires, tornadoes, and earthquakes. I have picked poor titles, had too much material to fit into my three-hour time slot, and offered my attendees way too much cold coffee. But for every problem that I had, I learned what to do and eventually my attendance grew. I started to relax, enjoy the seminar, and the dollars started to grow in my seminar account.

I promise that as soon as that first seminar is over, you will be starting to plan your next one. You will find that it is as much fun planning a new seminar as it is presenting your current seminar. Each seminar will become easier to design and you will lose your seminar stress and gain a sense of absolute enjoyment.

Resources

Bergman,Eric. 5 Steps To Conquer Death By Powerpoint. Petticoat Press Inc. 2012.

Gendelman, Joel. Virtual Presentations That Work. New York: McGraw-Hill. 2010.

Gitomer, Jeffrey. Social Boom! New Jersey: FT Press. 2011.

Handley, Ann and C.C. Chapman. Content Rules. New Jersey: John Wiley & Sons. 2012.

Hyatt, Michael. Platform: Get Noticed in a Noisy World. Nashville: Thomas Nelson. 2012.

Kapterev, Alexei. Presentation Secrets. Indianapolis, Indiana: John Wiley & Sons. 2011.

Meyerson, Mitch. Mastering Online Marketing. Entrepreneur Press. 2008.

Reynolds, Garr. PresentationZEN. Berkeley, California: New Riders. 2012

About the Author

Dr. Bill Wittich is a speaker, consultant and seminar leader.

For the past twelve years, Bill and his wife Ann, have traveled an average of 200 days a year conducting thousands of seminars. Their seminar schedule has taken them to all corners of the United States and through much of Europe.

His doctorate is from the University of Southern California where he continues to serve as a mentor to graduate students in the School of Policy, Planning, and Development.

Dr. Wittich has authored ten books in the association and non-profit field. His books are available through Barnes & Noble and Amazon.com. They are in print and e-book format.

Bill is a member of the Rotary Club of Laguna Sunrise in Elk Grove, California.

They enjoy living in Northern California, where they enjoy taking cooking classes, collecting antiques, and learning about California red wine.